MW00849757

ONE HELL OF A RIDE II

From the French Connection to Operation Southern Comfort

PIERRE "Pete" CHARETTE

LitPrime
"Your story is our priority"

LitPrime Solutions
21250 Hawthorne Blvd
Suite 500, Torrance, CA 90503
www.litprime.com
Phone: 1-800-981-9893

This is a true story. All the characters, names, incidents, organizations, and dialogue in this novel are true except for some names that are protected for security purposes.

Contact the author at pellijay@aol.com

Published by LitPrime Solutions   05/20/2022

ISBN: 978-1-955944-96-0(sc)
ISBN: 978-1-955944-97-7(hc)
ISBN: 978-1-955944-98-4(e)

Library of Congress Control Number: 2022909071

DEDICATIONS

This book is dedicated to my loving family, friends, and Law Enforcement Officers, whose support has kept me motivated to begin Volume II of One Hell of a Ride.

To my brothers Gill (RIP), John, Bernard, and Louis! Love you guys!

I also wish to say thanks to my loving wife Paula who encouraged me not to give up along with the encouragement from my kids and grandkids!

I personally want to thank my editor, Frank Sabina, and book designer, Dana Bree, for their continuous support and for making it possible to be such a success. This was not one man's effort but a team effort. I am honored to tell my story with your support and encouragement. The "Ride" continues for me with worldwide support such as yours. Enjoy PART II!

R.I.P. To all who have passed away while doing this important work. Special prayers to all of you.

AUTHOR'S NOTE:

Due to the nature of my 33 years in law enforcement work, I need to ensure that some people with whom I have worked and are still alive are protected from anyone wishing to harm them; therefore, I must protect their identity and safety first. Their names will be protected by using pseudo names. The accounts of the famous cases in which we were involved are real and not fabricated or enhanced in any way. I have nothing but pride for having been involved in one of the greatest historical cases ever made worldwide. Thank you, God, for protecting me from death on numerous occasions.

TESTIMONIALS
for One Hell of a Ride I

Dr. Carlton E. Turner, PH.D.,
Former Drug Czar to President Ronald Reagan, Deputy Assistant to President Ronald Reagan for Drug Abuse and Director of the White House Drug Abuse Policy

"In my 78 years of life, God has provided me many opportunities most of which a country boy from rural Alabama could not have dreamed, much less lived. Along the way from the farm to the White House, I met extraordinary people. One was Pete Charette. Pete is a natural storyteller and writer. As an instructor for the Bureau of Narcotics and Dangerous Drugs (BNDD) and the Drug Enforcement Administration (DEA) from 1970 to 1981, it was my privilege to meet key members of both organization from the agents on the street to the Directors and Administrators. From my vantage point, Pete was the best. His language skills allowed him to go places few could go. His natural ability to survive in the drug underworld, combined with an uncanny ability to communicate his experience provided us with an understanding of the dangers a drug enforcement agent faces each day. You may find Pete's experiences unbelievable but believe me they are real. Your view of drug enforcement agents will change."

B. Boykin Rose
Associate Deputy Attorney General of the United States Department of Justice (retired)

"If you want to experience vicariously the exhilarating and daring life of an undercover DEA agent with a storied career, look no further than this book. Pete Charette accomplished what few others could in the dark and sinister war against narcotics trafficking through sheer willpower, unflinching bravery and cunning. He possessed a singularity of purpose, integrity and vision coupled with an ability to lead a diverse group of federal, state and local law enforcement officials in a way that was not common at the time.

I had the privilege of serving as Associate Deputy Attorney General in the United States Department of Justice. In that role, I worked with many law enforcement professionals. I found them to be honorable people working in an admirable profession. Yet in life, there are always standouts. Pete was most assuredly one such person. His intellect, passion, fearlessness and leadership made him a powerful weapon in the fight against organized crime. Doing a good job satisfies most people. Pete was driven by a ferocity that commanded respect, awe and admiration, achieving unprecedented results. So for those of you who are drawn to stories of courageous people who win against all odds, who never despair and carry on, this book is for you."

John B. Brown III
Deputy Administrator (retired)
U.S. Drug Enforcement Administration

"Pete Charette has not only been a trusted colleague and Brother Agent – he was even once my boss – but for nearly half of a century, he has been a tremendous friend!

Many of us met Pete for the first time on that cold January morning in 1972 when we reported to the headquarters of the former U.S. Bureau of Narcotics and Dangerous Drugs (BNDD) at 14th and "I" streets in downtown Washington, DC. We were to become BNDD Basic Agent Training Class #23, and if we made it through training successfully, we would become Federal Narcotics Agents.

"Pete stood out right from the beginning. A bundle of French energy whose personality was as big as his smile, Pete became fast friends with everyone. Our classmates had backgrounds as diverse as any you could imagine. Some of us had prior law enforcement experience, many had been teachers, sales personnel, whatever—a few even had very mysterious backgrounds that no one ever talked about. Pete came to the BNDD academy after already having had a stellar career as a detective in South Florida, where he worked tough narcotics cases—and even tougher official corruption cases. In BNDD #23, Pete did what he always has done—he relied on his experience and perspective and reached out to give a helping hand to some of our classmates to make sure they made it through training.

"In his book, Pete takes us along as he works as a Special Agent to bring down some of the largest criminal organizations ever known. Nobody worked harder than Pete–not that Pete even had to work hard–not with all his experience, ingenuity and expertise. But I have always believed that Pete's true legacy–even greater than what he accomplished as a Special Agent–will be what he has done as a Supervisor and Manager to mentor, guide and support other Agents and Officers–just as he did back in basic training, to make certain that the job got done the right way, and that everyone went home safely in the end."

SAIC Thomas Cash
Retired Special Agent in Charge
Drug Enforcement Administration, Miami, Florida

"Pete Charette had a most interesting life and very interesting cases. More so than average agents because of time and circumstances surrounding his assignments. His assignments were aided by his ability to speak fluent French in a critical time. It was known in France and other countries in Europe, as the "Agent Provocateur" law and such activity by a French Police officer or Agent was viewed as totally illegal in French Courts. Actually, cases were not prosecuted when such activity occurred as the alleged "provoking agent's" conduct led to the acquittal of the heroin trafficker or any other criminal. The acquittal was valid inasmuch as the officer or Agent was" luring innocents to commit the crime of heroin production." DEA however could do the meetings, the surveillances, the visits and pose as anyone they could get away with pretending to be. So that is where Pete Charette came in and that is part of what you will read about in this book.

"So, to combat that heroin scourge, you needed a young French speaking man or woman to do what became known as the "Undercover" work because the French could not do the enticing informative work necessary to discover the crime of heroin trafficking. It was made for Pete Charette and he did it often and successfully working out of our Paris office. Fluent French was what made his undercover act believable. Plus, he looked like a young French criminal which made his act all the more successful.

"In my later career I too worked in Paris as Assistant Regional Director and Pete was still seen as the icon of the Paris office who began our success working with the French National Police. DEA would do what the French could not do, and DEA could testify in French Court as they were accredited to France through the Embassy. Without such undercover operations, the French would have been buried in heroin.

"Later in my career as I was the Special Agent in Charge of the Miami Field Division and assigned him to the Caribbean Offices where his French came into play in many of the French speaking islands. Just remember that truth is stranger than fiction. DEA Special Agents serving around the globe have had some amazing results not all of which have been categorized. Perhaps Pete's book with an amazingly true title will inform you of some of the cases that can now be revealed."

Special Agent Steve Murphy *(retired DEA)*
Co-Founders and Keynote Speakers, DEA Narcos

"Pete Charette is another of America's unsung heroes, someone that dedicated his life to protecting others as well as his country, someone who didn't ask for, nor seek attention or glory, someone who had a loving wife and family who understood when the call of the job had to come first. He was a DEA Special Agent who knew the job and proactively worked it, an Agent who set an example for others to follow, an Agent who became a leader and mentor, and an Agent who is my friend.

"In today's society, the word 'hero' is thrown around freely with little regard to the actions or circumstances involved. But Pete earned that title, although he'll never use that title or admit it. But isn't that one of the traits of a true hero?

If you want to learn what life as a DEA Agent can be like, the dangers, the excitement, staying focused on your mission, this is the book for you. Pete doesn't tell stories about what others did while he sat back and watched. He lays out firsthand knowledge of how he worked undercover in a seedy and violent world when any day could realistically be his last. This isn't Hollywood, this is real life from a man who lived it!!!

"I had the pleasure of working under Pete while stationed in Miami. His enthusiasm was contagious, his advice was sought, and we always knew he had our backs. Pete was instrumental in supporting me for assignment to Colombia. We maintained contact which resulted in us working on some of the first Colombian heroin cases. And of course, Pete was always there to support us in the Pablo Escobar investigation.

Pete, thanks for your commitment to duty and honor, and for always supporting us "baby" Agents!!! God bless you and your family my friend!"

Kenneth (Mac) McCarron
Retired Supervisory Special Agent
U.S. Drug Enforcement Administration
U.S. Department of Justice,
Miami Field Division, Miami, Florida

"I met Pierre "Pete" Charette in 1985, when I was a Special Agent with the United States Drug Enforcement Administration (DEA) in Miami, Florida. Having the opportunity to not only meet Pete, but to work for and with Pete was very instrumental and benefited me greatly in becoming a successful Special Agent and Supervisory Special Agent with the DEA. Pete recruited me to manage a multi-agency Ad Hoc Task Force responsible for the pursuit, investigation, arrests and convictions of significant co-conspirators responsible for the manufacture and distribution of marijuana throughout the State of Florida. The investigation proved successful and the experience and knowledge I acquired while I worked as Pete's Case Agent proved successful the rest of my 37 years in the field of law enforcement. The supervisor, partner and brother I was blessed to have in my life is Pete Charette, who has always honored, cherished and protected the shield he wore."

Kevin Studer
Program/Operations Manager
DSoft Technology Engineering and Analysis, Inc.

"It is rare in one's life that you come face to face with a real-life patriot. I have had such a privilege. Pete Charette has been one of if not my best friends for the last eight years - and I've never met a better human being. He has been a loving father, a dedicated husband, a brilliant storyteller, with a deep core of compassion and empathy, who's continually put himself in harm's way for his country, his community, and those he loves. Pete is a genuinely selfless man who's made an enormous impact in my life. It was an honor to have him in my wedding party. His stories about his time in the DEA were the kinds of things I thought were pure 'creative embellishment' when I first met him. But as I've gotten to know him, and talked with those that have known him, I've realized just how much of a wild ride his life has been. He has always been willing to pass on his stories, experiences, and wisdom in the most unassuming manner to not only myself but also to those that he works with in our company. I'm sure he's got a few more wild adventures in him—and I have no doubt they'll be one hell of a ride!"

Table of Contents

Table of Contents

Prologue

In One Hell of a Ride 1, I describe what led me to seek a Law Enforcement career. It covers nine years of unbelievable cases I worked from the beginning of my career to my recruitment by the Federal Bureau of Narcotic and Dangerous Drug to work undercover in Paris on the famous "French Connection" Investigation of the Corsican mob, in Marseille, France. They were responsible for manufacturing the best heroin in the world and purchased by the U.S. mob. My career transported me from the U.S. to undercover work throughout Europe and behind the Iron Curtain in Belgrade, Yugoslavia where my colleagues and I uncovered the first heroin lab in a Bloc Country. My first book is filled with dangerous cases and intrigue! The result of those nine years in book I, has been hailed by numerous reviews and is presently being considered to become a movie and television series.

This book will cover my return to the United States as a newly appointed resident agent in charge of The Colombia, South Carolina, DEA Office and as it turns out will involve more historical cases and drug seizures and the arrests of several prominent figures as well as threats to my life and my family. Most importantly, I will tell you about my involvement in a case named "Operation Southern Comfort" led by the Medellin family and Pablo Escobar. This case covered one and a half years of undercover investigations and was pronounced by the U.S. Attorney General of the United States as "the biggest cocaine conspiracy in the history of the United States" which resulted in the arrest of 52 defendants and dismantled a major U.S. mob organization based in Florida, Georgia, Tennessee, and North Carolina.

It will also cover my assignment in Washington, D.C. and final transfer to Miami as the Assistant Special Agent in Charge of the DEA Resident Offices in Florida and the Caribbean Islands.

I hope you will enjoy my crazy adventures, and that they will keep you excited as you read the sequel and my one hell of a ride!

PART ONE

NEW DUTIES, NEW CASES

1
Arrival State Side
New Resident Agent in Charge
Columbia, South Carolina

P rior to departure for my new post of duty in Columbia, South Carolina, I was instructed to meet my bosses in Miami.

On Monday morning, I walked into the new Miami office and reported to my new ASAIC David Connelly who was a good friend and a great boss. He said, "Pete, welcome back. Great to see you after five years! The RD John Van Diver (deceased) is waiting for us. Let us go in!"

Once inside, the RD stood and began welcoming me. "Pedro! How are you doing? I have been anxious to have you here! Congratulations on your quick appointment. When we got the call and filled in how it came about, Dave and I were elated that you had been chosen, and I fully supported this! Just want you to know, that we know you will make this office come to life. The RAIC (deceased) who retired had some issues and a different philosophy on making cases. Best I can describe it, was the old saying by some 'No cases, no problems! Lots of cases, big problems!' You will see that once you sit down with us and read up on the Office Administrative file." He continued, "Pedro, South Carolina is extremely political with lots of corruption, and you will have to watch your back. That is why we are glad that you are taking over! If you have any problems, you're covered by both of us, when you need us!"

"Thank you, Sir. I want you to know I appreciate your support! You both know me, and there's nothing more that I love than a good challenge!" I offered with a casual smile.

"Pedro, spend a few hours reading the file on the office and your ASAIC will bring you up to date. And among us, It's John, pal."

"You got it, John! Thank you and great seeing you!"

"Pete! Let's go upstairs!" Dave interjected.

Dave and I went to his office, and he began by saying. "Pete, first, the office is small, and you have, as far as I am concerned, the best secretary in DEA, Janice Goggans (deceased). I want to warn you though, Agent Norman Shumard (deceased), who is one of the best we have in the field, is disappointed that he was not selected to be the new RAIC and may be standoffish with you. Be prepared for a cold reception at first, but you and he will end up great friends after a while."

"Thanks for the heads up!"

"Take off your jacket, sit down at that table and go ahead and review your office Administrative Manual from the past year."

The manual was about four to five inches thick. Most were in-house copies from the previous RAIC to Agent Shumard along with normal monthly reports on drug trends neglecting his responsibility and liaison activities. "The thing that is disturbing to me was the communication from a boss to one agent! Done by memo in a two-man office? What kind of relationship existed between these two?" I commented to Dave.

I continued to study the manual and comment. "The RAIC had a different style of management, and this had become an issue that was hard to deal with! He was eligible to retire, and he submitted his retirement papers and retired!"

Norm became acting RAIC for the past few months and things had settled down. Once I had finished my reviews and briefing, I departed and was told to officially start work on the following Monday.

I called the office and Janice Goggans answered, "Hi, Janice, this is Pete Charette!"

"Mr. Charette! So good to hear from you. I have everything ready for you that you asked for and when are you arriving?"

"Thanks, Janice! I am arriving tomorrow and thank you for the hotel reservations you made for us."

"My pleasure. I'm getting a rental, I should arrive by 10:00 a.m., get my wife settled in, and will come to the office after lunch, around 2 p.m."

"Great. Norm and I will be waiting. Heard a lot about you through the ASAIC and your brother John!" Norm is not here; he is at SLED right now!"

"Okay, see you all soon!"

* * *

Columbia, SC was not new to me since it was where I took my military training in 1963. Upon arriving, I noticed that the town had grown, and we were able to find a home quickly within one month. My wife dropped me off at the office, which was located 15 minutes from downtown. The office was in a two-story building which housed several professional businesses.

DEA was on the second floor. The office consisted of 5 small areas, a small file room/evidence room, with an alarm system throughout the office, a communication center, front secretary/receptionist area with a plate glass window, a Xerox room, and an agent room for two people.

I entered the office and to my left standing up to greet me was Janice, the office secretary. "Mr. Charette! Finally, you made it safely. Welcome to Columbia."

"Janice, a pleasure to meet you. Glad to be here and look forward to working with you and Norm!"

"Thank you. Let me show you around, please!" I was given a brief tour after which Janice led me to Agent Norm Shumard who was sitting at his desk wearing a weak smile at first. He stood up as I approached him, and we both shook hands.

"Welcome to Columbia, Sir! Pleasure to meet you. Heard a lot about you!"

"Great meeting you. I also heard about you! All good, trust me! Just one thing I would like to say before we sit down and talk! That is that starting right now I am Pete to both of you, my name is not Doe Boy, and if we communicate, it will never be by memo. I read too many of them while going over the office file in Miami!" I hope you understand what I am saying and that policy from my predecessor no longer exists! Are we clear?"

Smiling! They both said together, "Yes, sir!"

"Good. Let us go to my office and talk! Janice, do you have any coffee here?"

"No. The previous RAIC (aka "Doe Boy") did not allow coffee pots in this office. We must buy it from the small canteen down the walkway. I will get it for you!"

"Here." I handed her money, "I'm buying for all of us. I'll put my stuff in my office in the meantime!"

"Thank You!"

* * *

Janice returned with the coffee, and we all sat in my office and began addressing them.

"Norm, I know that it's always tense when a new boss comes in and expectations have been changed when you had hopes to get this job and didn't get it! I am a very upfront guy, and you will quickly learn that I tell it like it is and will never go behind anyone's back. If I have something to say, I will say it and discuss it with you immediately. I am not perfect by any means, and I appreciate people who are up front and do not kiss the boss's ass! My management style is different than most others. I'm here to work together with you as a team and not to micromanage this office. You will learn amazingly fast that I am a case making person and love the action, and my job with you all is to put the ass holes in jail for drug trafficking!

"I know that you were hoping to get the position! I did not apply for this post. The administrator appointed me to this post. I hope that clarifies the matter. Trust me, I'm honored to work with you. I know that you have been here for the most part of your career and that the law enforcement community admires you and this office existed because of you!

"I have done my homework, and Janice, correct me if I am wrong, according to your case log, there is only one case in the books at this time while under the previous RAIC. Is that correct?"

"Yes, sir, and only two CI s (Confidential Informants!)."

"Norm, I have heard about your frustrations, and being held back from making more cases, etc. This is a new beginning for all of us. My policy is making cases, and I will support you 100% on this, and you and I will sit down tomorrow and develop a plan to start putting traffickers in jail!"

"Yes, Sir, uh, Pete!" he answered smiling.

"Any questions?"

"Pete, John would not allow me to make buys, without his permission first. What's your position on this?"

"Simple. It's your call. Just tell me what it's about, and I'll get you all the resources needed and help with surveillance for which you will be calling the shots! And if you need me to work undercover, I will do so, since you are well known! Money is no object. I told Miami that I will keep them posted on what is going on, but I call my own shots, which they totally agreed on."

"Pete, that sounds good to me."

"Pete, as the secretary, at times I have been asked by Miami to do some typing for them since we didn't have a large workload here. How do you feel about that!?"

"No, problem, but trust me, that won't last long. We will be busy very soon. Norm, I need for you to take me to my hotel. Chris and I have an appointment to look at a few houses today, if you wouldn't mind!"

"No problem. Better than that. Janice, give him the keys to the RAIC's car. It is parked out back, the blue Lincoln Continental. It has a radio in it and a floor button for the phone, hidden under the carpet. The keypad is behind the visor!"

"Great, you're in charge, Norm! If you need me, I am on beeper! See you all tomorrow. Oh! By the way! Are you still going to Big Boy for coffee at 7:00 a.m.? I will join you guys! If that is okay with you?" The look on their faces was priceless!

* * *

My first day went well, and I noticed after our talk that the body language seemed to change to a relaxed mood. Janice came in my office and quietly said, "Pete, Norm seldom gives his opinion to anyone. I just came out of his office, and he told me, 'This guy, isn't what I was expecting. He is upfront and speaks his mind and looks like we are going to be in for a change!'

I know him well, and you made an impression on him. You're off to a good start!"

"Thanks. He's a great agent from what I have heard, and I think we will all have one hell of a ride from here on!"

As I left the office, I felt good about the first meeting and knew that things would work out great and we would become a great team together. I realized that when I said to Norm that I would work undercover when needed, I observed his body language reacted, and he wore a surprised, curious look on his face. This indicated to me that I would address this concerned look with him in private. During this period in the 70's, there was some RAIC's, whose mentality was that "bosses don't work undercover." These were agents who were good at kissing ass with big bosses, and some identified as being afraid of their own shadows, i.e., cowards! (Among some of my colleagues, we would refer to them as great 'candidates' for a well-known federal agency of white-collar jobs.

At 7:00 a.m. I pulled up at Shoney's Big Boys for breakfast with the team. They were sitting with a couple U.S. marshals who were regulars and awfully close friends of our office. We returned to the office where the routine was to read the morning Teletypes from Washington, which informed us of the last 24 hours of arrests and seizures of drugs worldwide and any requests for action from us by U.S. offices. This was done in my office. Once we finished, I asked Norm to stay, and we began discussing the agenda. He had to introduce me to the Richland County Sheriff Dept. members, South Carolina Law Enforcement Agency heads, and Narcotic Bureau Agents, Lexington County Sheriff and narcotics agents.

I told Norm I was ready to go but wanted to ask him about his possible concerns about my working undercover. He looked at me amazed that I had picked up his reaction. I told him being able to read people saved my life on numerous occasions. I said, "Norm, don't ever be afraid to ask me anything. This way by being partners and friends, we can clear the air without having worries about one another!"

He responded laughing and said, "Damn! You shocked the hell out of me when you said that! Because there are RAIC's in this division that will bad mouth the hell out of you for doing that!"

"Norm, I am no better than you, and if the need arises for me to do that to put these SOBs in jail, then so be it! If they got a problem, let them address it with me, and they will get a swift response to GFY themselves. My office, my call!"

He started laughing, shaking his head, and said, "I know of two MFs that will confront you, and I can't wait! You will be revered by their agent and hated by them!"

"Norm, I appreciate your honesty and we will show them how cases are made in this state! I'm not looking for a fight and will try to work with them as a professional, but mark my word, I won't be told that I can't do UC work because I will stand my ground and back my Agent 110% always. Let's go meet our friends, Norm! Like the Chinese admiral said to his officers when they launched the attack on Pearl Harbor, 'I'm afraid we have awakened a sleeping giant' is what they will be told!" We both started laughing and left for our meeting.

* * *

The first stop was the Richland County Sheriff's Department located downtown Columbia, South Carolina. The sheriff was Frank Powell (deceased) who was highly respected.After spending an hour with him, he was extremely pleased with the relationship his department had with DEA thanks to Agent Norm Shumard. I advised him that our office will continue the relationship, that things will change, and we together will make an impact in this community to take swift action against drug organizations in this state. He welcomed me to the state and assured me along with his Chief of Detective Bureau that his department has their full cooperation. I was then introduced to Lt. McNeilly who was head of the Narcotics Bureau along with Detectives Robert Weir and Denis "The Snake" Craig. These Narcs were our best friends who had our backs 100%.

After receiving a briefing, we departed to the Lexington Sheriff's Department to meet the Sheriff and his narcotic agents Lt. Sonny Clark, Detectives Jim Matthews, and Tim Crocker. After being given a briefing, we were once again told that we had 100% cooperation when needed, and we all became great friends on and off the job.

Our last stop was The South Carolina Law Enforcement Department (SLED) whose Director Peter Strom was the most powerful figure in the state being compared to FBI Director J. Edgar Hoover. Meeting the chief was an experience, and he made it clear that he was in charge and wished me well in my position. I assured him that our great relationship with his Narcotics Bureau would remain solid, and that I would pursue with vigor the arrest and prosecution of individuals who operated illegally in the trafficking of narcotics regardless of their positions. He smiled and said, "Mr. Charette, I have been told that you were an extremely aggressive person, and we welcome you and look forward to continuing working with you in this fight. You have a good day, sir!" Norm and I then went to the narcotics office to meet everyone.

The LT. Buford Mabrey oversaw the 10-man unit and was highly respected by all. Throughout my assignment we became friends, having disrupted numerous smuggling organizations and politicians in the state. His supervisor was Sgt. Steve Smith who remains a good friend. The agents were Carlton Medley, Jim McClary, Murry Fant, and Bill Schaekel We all discussed what the drug situation was, and there was no doubt that South Carolina was one of the favorite places for marijuana smuggling on the Southeast Coast. Marijuana shipments arrived by ship and airplane off the coast. We were advised that 'the good old boys' (What we called the politicians) were very tight, and the secrecy of our operations had to be adhered too. Corruption was very prominent, and in four years we made a real impact on these organizations. Buford and I had a private discussion and agreed that the sharing of information was a must, and trust was established among ourselves that day. I advised him that I was here to do my job aggressively and that I demanded integrity and loyalty from my employees. We left feeling great from our meetings and were ready to make cases.

I decided with Norm that we needed to go to the U.S. Attorney's office to have him make introductions. We first went to meet Assistant United States Attorney Tommy Simpson. He was highly respected by everyone in his office and ran the Prosecution Attorneys group, which consisted at that time of 8 AUSA's. Tommy was approximately 5'11", a big muscular framed man, very pleasant, and always smoked a pipe.

Tommy said, "Been hearing a lot about you, and congratulations on your appointment. You have quite a reputation and aggressive style to make cases from what I have heard."

"Tommy, from what I have been told by Norm, you are looked upon as the best AUSA in the state, and I assure you that the relationship will continue. We will ensure that we keep you and your attorneys posted on all case that we open to ensure that we get a 100% conviction rate."

"Pete, you and I will get along great because I feel the same way. Let's go and meet the USA (United States Attorney) Tom Lydon. He's waiting to meet you."

I was introduced to his secretary as we entered the office. She knocked on a glass-frosted door which Mr. Lydon then opened and introduced himself right away. "Mr. Charette, I've been looking forward to meeting you!"

It's my pleasure, sir, and from now on call me Pete since we will be working very closely together."

"Pete, I fully agree, and based on my sources with the Department of Justice in D.C., you have quite a record for making cases. I'm glad we got you here. South Carolina is an immensely popular state for importation of marijuana, cocaine, and heroin. We have also the beginning of methamphetamine labs and sales which is a real concern to the community."

"Tom, I have met with the chiefs of police and sheriffs already, and they express the same concerns. I am an extremely aggressive enforcer against drug trafficking and corruption, and will not back down, regardless of someone's status in the state. I have several plans that I will be working with the law enforcement community within the next 30 days and plan on hitting the ground at full speed."

He looked at me directly and said, "I'm glad to hear this and welcome to South Carolina."

"Thank You. And I look forward to a great relationship with you and your staff."

We left Mr. Lydon's and went to meet the U.S. Magistrate Charles Gambrell. Judge Gambrell was in his late 50's about 5'10" and had a deep southern drawl when he spoke. We hit it off well, and he supported our efforts. He was the best magistrate I ever had the pleasure to work with in my career. We spent about 30 minutes in his office and left to meet with the Richland County Solicitor James Anders.

Mr. Anders' office was in the center of town. Norm had briefed me, advising that Mr. Anders was extremely respected by the law enforcement community and his office, enjoying putting drug traffickers in jail. They referred numerous violators who wanted to cooperate for reduction of charges against them to Norm.

As we walked into the solicitor's office, the secretary greeted us and said, "Hi, Norm. Jim got your message, and he's waiting for you and Mr. Charette! Mr. Charette, welcome to Columbia, sir!"

"Thank you and call me Pete."

When we walked in, Mr. Anders was already standing and said, "Pete, Jim Anders. Pleased to meet you."

Standing next to him was Solicitor Richard Harpootlian , Mr. Anders was approximately 5'8", slim build, 175 lbs. brown hair. Dick was in his late 30's, slim, 5'9" and had a southern accent. After introductions, we sat down, and they both expressed how great the relationship was between our office and theirs. This was of course due to Norm's great liaison with this office.

At times, small cases were adopted by Mr. Anders' office and their conviction rate was outstandingly high. This friendship made a big difference. The arrest rate climbed rapidly with the cooperation we had, making an impact in the community. Upon concluding our meeting, we headed back to the office.

Norm, Janice, and I sat down and after going over our meetings agreed that the cooperation was there, and it was now up to us to meet with the ground undercover officers and supervisors to strategically identify the source of supply, street dealers, aircraft smugglers and municipal and county airports, etc. Once we agreed to a plan of attack, it was full speed ahead!

Based on my meetings, it was obvious that the financial

support to the law enforcement agencies focusing directly and historically to uniform patrol divisions, the detective bureau, i.e., homicide division, robbery division, juvenile division and the vice/narcotics squads was not considered a high priority budget allocation, which should be a must to make and break the major distribution of drugs in cities and counties in the state.

We all agreed that I had to get additional drug-buy money to be able to infiltrate the supply sources. This ride was not going to stop, and together we could cause hell. The drug traffickers were in for a surprise once we go on the attack together!

"Norm! What's the money limit that doesn't need approval from Miami?"

"Pete, the established policy is $1500. Anything above that needs permission and justification! We call this stupid childish policy "Mother May I?"

"Guess what? This is going to change, watch me! I am calling Dave Connelly. Who in the Hell came up with that amount? No wonder cases are being delayed and not made. That is Micromanaging and RAIC's should have authority to approve up to $5K, without approval from management?" We walked into the office, and I asked Janice to get Mr. Connelly on the phone for me.

"Norm. Come on in. I want you to hear this.

"Pete, Dave is on line 1 for you!"

"Thanks, Janice! Hi, Dave! I need to run a few things by you if you got time."

"Sure, Pete. What's up?"

"Dave, Norm, and I have met with the Chief of Police and Director of SLED and U.S. Attorney. Everything went very well, thanks to Norm setting this up. The result was extremely positive, and we all agreed that cooperation was a must, and I requested their support in providing one agent from their department to work directly from our office informally as an Ad Hoc Task Force to make an impact in South Carolina in my area of responsibility.

They all agreed and fully supported this concept. I advised them that all arrests and seizures of drugs would include a joint press release which they fully supported."

"Good Job, guys. I like this concept, Pete. Anything else?"

"Yes, Dave! I asked Norm about what the Buy-Drug Money policy was, and he told me that $1500 was the max! Dave, I can't believe that HQ has put this out, I'm used to $5K, and need to have this changed. Trust me, I am a big boy, and you know that I can produce results. I don't need to keep hounding you for permission for money. During FBN days the budget was tight, but times have changed. Tell the boss that the 'Frenchman' is ready to make his office number one in the U.S."

"Pete, point made! Will tell John that I fully agree, and you will receive the okay within 24 hours, Give them Hell my friend!" "Thanks Dave, I won't let you down. I'll keep you posted, sir!"

"Okay, Norm, that was easy. Thanks for your support. Let us lock up for the day and go home. Tomorrow, we have a group meeting with our new partners."

2
The Attack on SC Drug Traffickers Starts
1977

M onday morning's first order of business was to review the teletypes sent to the office by DEA offices and HQ, which varied from. case assistance request, policy changes, vacancy announcements of positions to applications for transfer to domestic offices or overseas positions. Once this was done, I said to Norm, "Can you call Lt. McNeely of Richland County SO, Supervisor Steve Smith of SLED, and Sgt. Sonny Clark of Lexington County and see if they can come meet with us at 2:00 p.m. to put into action our team plan?"

"Got it, Pete! I talked with them over the weekend, and they are waiting for you to get this going!"

"Great, and for your info, Dave Connelly called me and advised me we had a green light from the boss that $5K was approved and for us to 'Kick ass.'" I informed him laughing."

"Man, that's the best news I've had, and I appreciate what you did. Unfortunately, our previous boss didn't have the gonads to accomplish this," Norm said smiling and giving a thumbs up sign.

At 2 p.m. everyone showed up with smiles on their faces, and Janice said, "I will hold all calls for you." Then she closed the door.

The meeting lasted one hour, and it was agreed that we

would all contact our confidential sources and have them set up buys with the known suppliers of heroin, marijuana, LSD, methamphetamine along with its labs. SLED advised me that Agent Murry Fant would be working at this office and coordinate the case for the state bureau. Detectives Billy Watson and Dennis Craig (deceased) were assigned by Richland County SO; Detective Jim Matthews was assigned by Lexington County SO. These were the best and we still all remained friends for life. I advised all of them that we had full authority up to $5K for purchase of undercover buys, and this was praised by all since their drug-buy budget was extremely low and hampered their case making with the "big guys." I was elated that we all supported doing this as a trusted team and things were about to change quickly!

Upon arriving to my new assignment, I had done some background research and discovered that for years South Carolina was being used as a port of entry for the most sought drug on the market at that time, marijuana. The drug came mostly from Mexico and Jamaica and a shift had occurred and estimates indicated that approximately 30,000 tons, worth around $40 billion came to the U.S. from Colombia, South America, with about half of it landing in South Carolina.

The favorite method of most of the transportation was by boat, since SC geographical coastline was ideal with creeks and inhabited islands. The Marijuana was transported by freighters from Colombia carrying as much as 100,000 pounds at a time and offloaded to small boats, normally 200 miles at sea, and some by small planes and four-engine DC-4s to rural airports or farming properties. This caused problems to law enforcement who failed to be properly funded and were out- manned and out-equipped.

The existing laws against these infractions were not severe enough and if caught, the penalty was considered a misdemeanor charge carrying a maximum penalty of 5 years and /or a $5,000 fine. Marijuana smuggling was an ideal drug to import through this state.

Our work was cut out, and we needed to be well coordinated and have a trusted team, sharing intelligence together. The key to our success proved that this could be accomplished, and the end results spoke for themselves as the situation unfolded.

I have selected the top cases made with our team, which are extremely historical in nature with action and intrigue. Without a team effort, we would have never been able to arrest the major traffickers, police officers and politicians. My life and family were threatened on numerous occasions, and you will get a true sense of what it is like to be in this type of career to serve this country proudly.

3
Significant Joint Cases
Columbia, South Carolina
1977 - 1981

DC-6 Marijuana Seizure 33,000 LBS (14-16 Tons) Florence, SC 12-31-1977 Street Value $9,500,000

It was New Year's Eve at the office, and I was working on paperwork when Murry Fant came into my office and said, "Pete, Florence Airport is on the line and said that they had a DC-6 aircraft that just landed for refueling. They said they just popped up on the radar near Jacksonville and requested clearance to land for refueling!"

"Murry, get the tail number, and we will run it on our system right away." I then notified our secretary. "Janice, get in here now please and run this aircraft tail number on NADDIS right away!"

"Yes, sir."

"Murry, tell the tower not to clear them for takeoff!"

"Got it!"

"Pete, NADDIS indicate it's on alert for possible drug smuggling!"

"Thanks, Murry! Call the sheriff's office in Florence and ask them to go and detain all passengers. We're on our way now and not to board the AC until we get there!"

"Roger that! Let us go now!"

"Janice, radio Norm and have him head to Florence Airport

ASAP!"

Murry and I left the office and blue lighted on the Interstate while Murry alerted the SC Highway Patrol that we were blue lighting to Florence at a high-speed!

"Pete, this is Norm. Fill me in!"

"Norm, we got a hit on a DC-6 refueling at Florence Airport, came in under radar in Jacksonville. We got the SO at the airport detaining the flight crew!"

"Great, just got word those agents from Charleston U.S. customs are on their way now!"

"Okay, will be waiting for you at the office there!"

"Murry, want to bet that customs will claim this as their case?"

"Pete, no way! It will be interesting!"

Before long, we arrived at the airport while the sheriff and his detectives along with marked patrol vehicles had surrounded the plane. Officers were detaining three individuals at the jet port. Sheriff William Barnes greeted Murry, and then he introduced me to him.

The sheriff then got to business at hand. "Pete, thank you for calling us quickly to detain these guys."

"Sheriff, pleasure to meet you and have you on board with us!"

The sheriff said, "let's walk over to the plane and see what you think of the smell coming from this. It's grass!"

The three of us walked underneath the plane. And we all immediately said "Damn! This SOB smells like a giant marijuana field!"

"Sheriff, can you have your team get a search warrant based on probable cause that this plane is loaded with marijuana based on the intense smell?

"You got it Pete, He approached his detectives, and they left to get the search warrant."

We went inside the Jet Port and sitting were the three suspected pilots.

Norm had just arrived with Dennis Craig, and I asked him to work with Murry and Dennis and the SO guys once the SW got here and boarded the plane to let us see what quantity we have.

Sheriff Barnes advised that the tower operators asked the pilot when the plane approached the airport for his plane ID number, the pilot would not give his proper ID and would only say that he was a DC-6 pilot! Further checks by the tower manager indicated that when they called Jacksonville FAA Tower operators, they were informed by them that the plane flight had originated in the Bahamas!

U.S. Customs arrived at the airport and advised me that they were charging the crew with smuggling marijuana into the U.S. I advised them that they were under investigation by DEA and that we were going to continue this investigation and appreciated them for charging them. A search of the plane disclosed that the plane had 33,000 lbs. of marijuana. This was the largest drug find in the History of South Carolina. The investigation continued for an additional six months.

The Defendants were as follows:

- Alan Aruda, 46, a millionaire residing in Ft. Lauderdale was sentenced in Federal Court in Florence, SC court to 10 years in prison and fined $15,000.
- Lawrence Rosenthal, 52, multi-millionaire owner of a large real estate firm in New York City, was sentenced to 5 years and fined $15,000.
- J.P. "Jim" Hollingsworth, 48, of Miami and Roberto Hernandez, 31, of Ft. Lauderdale were both sentenced to 5 years. A third man Herman Hernandez, Brother of Roberto, 33-year-old living in Colombia, South America failed to return for trial.

This case was historical in nature and was successfully executed by all cooperating parties. It resulted in the swift apprehension of the largest seizure of marijuana in the History of South Carolina.

Largest Seizure of Marijuana, in South Carolina 33,000 lbs.

Case Name — Jerome Upchurch

Arrested: Jerome Upchurch Heroin organization, Camden, South Carolina 1979-1981

Largest heroin investigation in South Carolina

Charges: One Criminal Enterprise Indictment Conspiracy to import of heroin to Philadelphia as well as Camden, Columbia, Lancaster, and Rock Hill in South Carolina.

Arrested: 17 Defendants after 2-year investigation.

Approximately 87 lbs. of heroin were delivered to South Carolina, worth approximately $90 million street value.

Charges: Fourteen defendants charged with conspiracy to distribute heroin, Federal Court.

Participating Agencies: DEA, Camden Police, SC, Camden Solicitor & Investigator, South Carolina Narcotics agents (SLED), Richmond County Sheriff's Department Narcotics Bureau, US Attorney Office, Columbia, SC

The beauty of being in the narcotic investigative work is that you never know what a new day at work will bring!

"Pete," Janice said walking into my office, "there's an Investigator from Camden, SC asking to meet with you. Can he come in?"

"Absolutely," I answered as I stood up to greet him.

"Mr. Charette, I'm Boykin Rose," he said while reaching out to shake hands.

"Boykin, pleasure to meet you. Have a seat." I grabbed the chair next to his.

Facing each other I saw that he was young, in his late 20s, muscular build and appeared to weigh 185, casual dress with great friendly smile and immediately likeable. "What brings you here to our crazy fun world?"

"Well, from what I hear, you have quite a career full of wild and crazy worldwide experiences as an expert in the heroin world! I was told by my police colleagues that you could help me with some info on some dope I bought yesterday in Camden?"

"Thanks for the compliment, Boykin. I will do my best. Tell me about yourself first! I always like to know about who I'm dealing with?"

"I am working as chief investigator for the Assistant Solicitor Bill Tetterton in Camden, SC. I have been doing this for several years. I love my job and do some undercover work and have been involved in a few shootings, been hurt a couple times, but that's part of the job!" He paused and laughed. "Last night I had an informant of mine arrange a heroin buy for me. I bought a load–15 dime bags of heroin, packaged in clear plastic bags wrapped with rubber bands!" He reached into his sports jacket pocket, pulling out the package.

"How much did you pay for the load?"

"Two hundred," he said to me. The reason for the price being high was that this was not your typical low percentage and could be cut numerous times for street sales. He told me his man in Philadelphia could do weight at any time. I need your help on this because I told him I wanted to buy an ounce for sure to see if he's lying to me!"

"Good move and quick thinking. You and I can work together! Ok, let me look at it and test it!"

I pulled out an ampule test tube from my pocket, which I always carried to test heroin when working in an undercover role! I unwrapped the load and took one of the dime bags, opened it and took out of my pocket, my faithful friend my Swiss army knife, and popped open the glass ampule and took a tip of the white heroin with the knife and dropped it in the ampule. BAM! BAM! To my amazement, the days of the French Connection brought me back to life in France!

"Holy Crap, Boykin, one more test and I think you have hit a jackpot source!" I dipped my finger into the open package and rubbed the bleach white heroin powder gently between my thumb and index finger hoping I was right that it would be smooth as silk. Bingo! "Boykin! All I can say is this shit, I am willing to bet is at least 80%. It has no grit like Asian heroin, a silky smoothness and this, to my best judgement, is French heroin. With your permission I would like to send this Overnight Express to our Miami laboratory for immediate analysis?"

"Pete, you got my full attention and cooperation, and can Norm take me to the nearest post office now?"

"Janice, please ask Norm to come here right away."

"Got it."

In a flash Norm appeared. "Norm, I need for you to take Boykin to the post office and package his evidence for Overnight Express to the Miami Lab for immediate analysis of this suspected heroin! I'll fill you in, looks like Boykin got one hell of a case with French heroin. He has got a major conspiracy going! By the way, I know that Jim Anders budget is low for Narcotics buys. How in the hell did you come up with the money to buy this and order an ounce which will most likely cost $2500 to $5K if I'm right?"

Norm, looking at me with a smile, said to Boykin, "Go ahead, shock him!"

"Pete, I can see no one told you about me yet! I use my own personal money for the buys I make, since our budget can't afford it," he said laughing!

"WTF! Are you crazy? Using your own money? Pal, it is mighty nice of you. I will reimburse you. This is your case, and we will take it to top together!"

"I am with you, Pal, but I will not take your money. You see, I am independently wealthy and don't take any salary except one dollar a year for tax purposes."

I was stunned to say the least and we all had a good laugh!

Boykin advised us that he would make arrangement with his source to meet and buy an ounce of heroin and pick a location for the buy. In the meantime, we would get phone records to trace calls to Philadelphia from this source and identify hopefully other dealers and plan to make buys from them.

"Okay! How about doing lunch together so I can get to know you better, Mr. Rose?"

"You're on! Let's go, my treat!"

After lunch, the heroin was sent to the Miami lab.

I received a call the next day from our chemist, advising me that the heroin was 82% pure and had all the marking of French heroin. I immediately notified Boykin and told him to set up the buy as soon as possible for tomorrow around 1:00 p.m. I also told him to call Norm with the details for the meet, and that he would meet with him with the surveillance team tomorrow.

I went to Norm's office and briefed him and Billy Watson on the lab results! Norm almost fell off his chair and yelled, "Holy shit! There is going to be some dead SOB's if they shoot up! We need to move fast on this. So far Boykin said he had bought from numerous sources. Billy, Murry, and I will hook up with Boykin in the morning, and I will draw from Janice $3000 for the buy!"

"Great, tell Boykin to have it go down at a local restaurant, not anywhere else. Ask Boykin also for copies of his file on this and hopefully, he has obtained phone records so far. If not, ask him to get Solicitor Tetterton to subpoena all phone records for these scumbags."

"Roger that! This has priority over anything else!"

"You got that right. Also tell Boykin to advise the source that he wants to get a kilo and meet the supplier to discuss business with him while I fly to Philly to meet and pick up the package, and that if he arranges this, there's a $1K bonus for him and all future buys. This will make this guy happy, and I guarantee he will set it up, mark my word!"

"Man! That is a new one! Never heard that line before!"

"Norm, it works every time that I have used that bonus trick! It makes them drool at the mouth! Okay, be careful tomorrow and remember if anyone must die, it's them not you. Keep me posted!" Norm and the guys were pumped up and so was I.

Janice came into my office and closed the door. "Permission to speak." I began to laugh. "I just want to tell you that I have been here for a few years, and I have never seen Norm, Billy and Murry so pumped up and excited since you came here! These guys have expressed to me how pleased they are to be working with you."

"Thank you, Janice, for your honesty and I assure you, I feel the same way about the group. You have helped me into making them confident with my style of management and I owe you a lunch tomorrow."

"Thanks, Pete! Proud to help and being part of the team! Since your arrival, you have kept me informed on everything that is occurring, which was never the case with the previous boss! Thank you and let us get back to work! Oh, don't forget lunch is on you!"

"I was hoping you would forget it! Damn!" I just laughed.

* * *

Boykin made the buy and the suspect agreed to arrange a meeting with Upchurch, who agreed to sell a kilogram of heroin to Boykin in Philadelphia. I contacted our Philadelphia DEA Office and briefed them on our case and was advised that they doubted that Upchurch had that kind of weight to sell.

So, Boykin and I flew to Philadelphia and surveillance arrangements were made for him to meet with Upchurch at his Bar Club to make the purchase. Boykin made the purchase and discussed future orders with him then left with the package in hand and returned to the office where we handed the kilogram to the case supervisor. The Deputy Director was shocked and could not believe we had made this buy. Everyone was overjoyed, and Boykin and I looked at each other with smiles.

As a result of this case 14 defendants were charged in Federal Court for conspiracy to distribute heroin. Upchurch was charged with heading a criminal enterprise consisting of five or more from which he derived a substantial income by selling heroin in Philadelphia, Camden and Columbia, SC.

The maximum Penalty for Conspiracy and each possession charges are not more than 15 years, or not more than $25,000 fine or both, plus a minimum three-year special parole term.

We were able to prove that this ring was responsible for bringing approximately 85 pounds of Heroin (valued at $20 million street value) to South Carolina during a four-year period. This heroin investigation was the largest in the state of South Carolina's history!

This teamwork of Officers' effort was recognized by presenting them with DEA awards presented by me.

Bottom Row –L/R Investigator Boykin Rose; Camden Police Chief W.R. Williams, Detective Albert Watson, Richland County Sheriff's Department; Assistant Solicitor William Tetterton; Officer Tommy Moore, Camden Police Department. Present at the Award Ceremony were Mayor James Anderson, Council Members Harvey Clark, W.

Bratton DeLoach, Frank Goodale and Clifton Alexander.

Note: Boykin Rose later became Associate Deputy General of the United State at the Department of Justice.

Case Name — Kenneth Jerry Haney

Arrested: Kenneth Jerry Haney, member of the Zasoff Boys, OCT.10/1978

Charges: Distribution and sale of cocaine, 5 ounces valued at $7,200, Possession of marijuana valued at $90,000.

Participating Agencies: DEA, Richland County SO. SLED, and Richard Harpootlian Solicitor Richland County, S.C.

This case made in 1979 is being mentioned because it shows that no one of popularity is immune from prosecution. The case started on information from a confidential source that Haney was selling large quantities of cocaine in South Carolina.

The informant introduced a DEA agent to Haney who was 27 years old and had achieved fame in the Country Music World. He had the honor with his band who had been asked to play for President Jimmy Carter's daughter's wedding in May of 1977. According to the source, Haney only sold to friends.

"Norm, Pete, Lt. McNeely is here and has a cocaine case and needs one of us to work undercover. The suspect is Country Western singer, Jerry Haney of the group the Zasoff Boys.

Pete, how are you doing? Glad to see that no one has shot you yet!" Mac snickered. "The word I'm getting from sources is that there's a new sheriff in town and he and the cops are kicking ass, big time!"

"Mac, that's a real compliment, and I appreciate the feedback. But we have just begun, my friend. Mac, give us what your source advised about Haney."

Mac said, "Haney is doing his weight, and our source told him that his friend wanted 5 oz. of coke! Haney advised the cost would be $7,200 which was agreed too. We can do it on the 10th at his home?"

Okay," I replied. "Norm, get the funds from Janice! And do it today. Tell everyone to come in, and Mac, it's your show. You know the layout of the place. Murry, you and Billy and the Snake, copy all the bills with Janice once we brief everyone!"

Everyone came in and Mac briefed all of us in 45 minutes. Janice and the boys verified the money count and copy of the bills.

The surveillance team was in place and the UCA (undercover agent) and the CI (confidential source), were observed entering the house. As planned the UCA was to meet and greet, show the money, ask to see the 5 oz., and checked it by doing a test! Once confirmed, he let Haney know that he would need an additional 6 oz. next week same time. Our agent and the CI were observed coming out of the residence, after which Haney was handcuffed and placed under arrest by our agent.

Haney was asked permission for a search of his residence, for which he fully cooperated.

Records of his drug business indicated that in 1977 his drug enterprise had made him $150,000. A review of his record was shown to the judge and not mentioned for release to the media. The record showed names of South Carolina citizens from all walks of life helped us to identify and arrest some affluential people that were mentioned in this book!

Haney appeared before Judge Sidney Floyd of the Richland General Session Court and pled guilty to all three charges. Judge Floyd sentenced Haney to 10 years for distribution of cocaine, ten years for second- and third-degree charges of possession with intent to distribute cocaine and possession of marijuana. Several people appeared before the judge asking for mercy. Despite the pleas for mercy from family, admirers and state officials, Judge Floyd imposed a flat 10-year sentence saying, "It gives me no pleasure at all. The problem with young people today is that they break the law, and their dearest and most cherished loved ones suffer." He concluded with, "But I'm not one who likes to lecture."

I commented to the media: "We are very pleased with the sentence that the judge handed down. We feel it will have an impact if his case and popularity are taken into consideration by the Department of Correction, that will be total discrimination against other prisoners who have been convicted of the same offense, and to me it would be a disgrace. He should be treated equally like the rest of them.

This case demonstrated that no favoritism was given to this individual who refused to cooperate with us. No one is above the law!

Case Name — FT. Jackson US Army Military Camp, Columbia, SC -1979

Arrested: Phillip Glymph – 34 Years Old – Unemployed
Charges: Sale of marijuana, possession of marijuana with intent to distribute, sale of cocaine, sale of dangerous drugs, conspiracy to distribute cocaine and marijuana
Arrested: Levi Isaac-26 years old. Student, 1535 Brookhurst Court, Columbia, SC
Charges: Sale of marijuana, Sale of dangerous drugs, Conspiracy to distribute cocaine and marijuana
Arrested: Robert Lee Jones- 21years old, 138th Military Police Command Ft. Jackson, SC
Charges: Simple possession of marijuana
Arrested: Chaspert Felton, 35, U.S. Army Supply Sergeant Ft. Jacksons, SC 5851 Palms Apartment, Columbia, S.C.
Charges: Sale of marijuana
Participating Agencies: DEA, US MILITARY CID, Richland County Sheriff's Department, Deputy Assistant Solicitor Richard Harpootlian for the Fifth Circuit Solicitor's Office, Columbia, SC

Not only did we work with state and local law enforcement in

Columbia SC, but I also established Liaison with the U.S. Military Police Criminal Investigation Division (CID) and together we Investigated and identified local sources of supplier to our military troops.

Working at the office, we had a visit from military investigators who requested our assistance in arresting local and military soldiers selling marijuana, pills and cocaine to military soldiers assigned to Ft. Jackson Base.

"Good morning! Please come and sit down. Well, it looks by the three of you, that we will be working together!"

"(*Names withheld*) Yes, Sir! We have been involved for close to a year in receiving information that some of our military troops have been buying on-base and off-base marijuana, cocaine, and pills! We finally were able to infiltrate this organization by bringing in a military police officer to work undercover on these suspects. We were not able to use our UC agents, since one of the suppliers was an MP of the 138th Military Police Command at Ft. Jackson!"

"Sounds like you have worked hard to identify these individuals, and we will assist you in getting the SOB'S taken down on conspiracy charges, the sooner the better! Janice! Get Norm to come in please!"

In no time Norm entered the room. "What's up, Boss?"

"You all know Norm?"

"Yes, Sir!" they replied.

The CID explained their case to Norm, and with a smile Norm said, "Gentlemen, we will prioritize this investigation immediately! I will contact Richland County Lt. McNeely and we together will start using your UC agent to make buys from these fine upstanding business pieces of shit." They all had a good laugh. I could tell by Norm's excitement that he was piped up for this!

"Gentlemen, rest assured that we will together take them down hard!"

"Sir, it's an honor to have had your support, and rest assured it will remain strong!"

"Thank you, Sir. Norm will take you to his office and get the information, and Lt. McNeely is on his way over so you can all plan your operation, and I will be there with you on this one too! It is always our policy to immediately assist our military, whenever there is information like this."

* * *

This brought back memories of when I was working in Paris. I received a phone call from a military CID agent who worked in an undercover role in Amsterdam who advised me that a night club owner was trying to blow his cover by telling other nightclub owners that he suspected him as being a U.S. agent. Nick, my boss, told me to plan a visit to this SOB as soon as possible with the team. The following summary reviews our visit:

In my first book, My CID UC contact in Amsterdam needed my assistance immediately because a local sex nightclub owner was spreading stories to the local club managers that our CID man was possibly an undercover agent for the U.S. His life was being endangered! And I Immediately got the okay from my European directors to pay this so-called gentleman, a U.S. mobster, a covert visit! The team consisted of my bodyguard, "The Hammer," The "Don," (deceased - great friend of all), Walter Pardean, the Don's bodyguard, Vernon, and I, "Canadian Boss" Pierre.

Upon arrival, the "Don" was dressed in a black suit, black shirt, white tie, smoking a cigar and looked like the Original Godfather escorted by "The Hammer" along with the rest of us. The CID agent walked up to the entrance at which time the doorman, a burly individual, put out his left arm across "The Hammer" who responded to his threat with a smile and the fastest upper cut, dropping him to the ground like a lead bullet! He was out like a light! He then stepped over him smiling and opened the door for all of us. The owner was sitting at a guest table in front of the stage with two of his waiters and turned around seeing our group!

He was in shock mode as we approached!

CID UC said, "Henry, I want you to meet my U.S. and Canadian family bosses, and their employees. They would like to have a talk with you, so please remain seated."

"Walter," Henry started extending his hand, "pleased to meet you, my friend! I am here to pay you a visit to thank you for all your merchandise that my friend Paul has been buying from you for us. As he leaned forward, he continued, "I hear we have a problem with your mouth, spreading nasty information! That Paul is a U.S. agent? This is extremely dangerous for his safety and for my marketing business in Canada and the U.S. I assure you–and you have my word– that he is legit, and I would like to invite you with us to visit your club manager's friends and reassure them that your source of information was proven wrong and is now swimming somewhere in your beautiful canals! (Walt was so convincing that it took everything in our power from bursting out laughing. This was right out of a movie scene!).All three of them looked scared as hell!

Henry responded immediately with an apology and ordered drinks for everyone. "Please, rest assured that your friend is safe, and I would love to take you around and introduce you all to my business associates."

"Great, that sounds wonderful! Our cars are out front, and you direct our chauffeur to these clubs!" As we came out, our wonderful doorman was holding the door open. He was looking pale and had a beautiful red chin all swollen along with a bleeding lip! The boss gave him a $100 bill for his delightful manners.

We completed our evening around 4:00 a.m. and returned to Paris all laughing and proud of the great reception by our guest.

As the saying goes "We Serve to Protect!"

Walter and I worked together again posing as Canadian mobsters in Belgrade, Yugoslavia. We made the biggest heroin case in a bloc country, resulting in the first seizure of a heroin lab operation. The entire story can be found in of *One Hell of a Ride 1*.

Our operation of undercover buys lasted three weeks. The UC personally observed buys from military basic training soldiers and regular soldiers. During this time frame, from observations by the UC and surveillance team, over 100 cars came to the residence of the main source of supply, Phillip Glymph.

The arrest was made on a Wednesday morning when agents armed with search warrants and arrest warrants, conducted a raid at the residence owned by Phillip Glymph, 34 years of age, located at 1733 Morning Glow Lane, Columbia, SC. Seized were drugs and $4000 in cash.

The reason this case was significant was to show that our cooperation to assist extended beyond state and local agencies. When I was transferred to Atlanta a few years later, the military CID, presented me with a plaque awarded for my assistance to the MP/CID units.

At the formation of our Informal Task Force, we worked together in identifying suspected long time drug trafficking gangs in our area of responsibility. The leaders of these organizations were identified, and the lengthy surveillances of them and phone records we collected helped us identify possible buyers and members of the organization. These apprehensions and the recruiting of cooperative sources helped us to make introductions to the head of the trafficking organization. Subsequently, we began to infiltrate these organization, and one of my agents with an informant was introduced to two major cocaine suppliers:

Case Name — William Jeffers

Arrested: William Jeffers 36 years old. Columbia, SC 1979.

Charges: Possession with intent to distribute cocaine. Conspiracy to distribute cocaine.

Arrested: Donaghey B. Corder, Jr. Columbia, SC

Charges: Possession with intent to distribute cocaine. Conspiracy to distribute cocaine. Possession of a firearm

Participating Agencies: DEA, Lexington County Sheriff's

Department, SLED, Richland County Sheriff's Dept., Department of Health and Environmental Control.

Seized: 1.2 kilograms of cocaine purchased for $24,000; street value $100,000

This investigation took two days of work, and Jeffers agreed to deliver a kilogram of cocaine to a DEA undercover agent, at a restaurant parking lot in Cayce, SC, which is adjacent to Columbia, SC. The arrest was made by 12 law enforcement agents and officers.

Both subjects were arrested without incident. Discovered inside the vehicle was a fully loaded .45 caliber automatic pistol on the front seat along with 18 ounces of cocaine.

This was the biggest drug bust ever made in Lexington County history according to Sheriff James Metts.

Our team was becoming very effective. As we continued making cases in the Midlands and Northern SC, we became the talk of law enforcement and almost daily we made headlines in the news media world of SC. I could list more cases, but I will end my stories with two most significant cases made which tied each other with local, state, and federal politicians resulting in state politicians conspiring to have my family and I killed!

4
Claire Manors Madame
Lexington County, South Carolina

D rug cases began increasing at a rapid rate because of our joint inter-agency investigation, Informal Task Force. In a ten-month period in 1977, our two-man office went from 2 cases to 34 cases with 161 arrests. This included substantial arrests of major trafficking organizations and traffickers identified as Class I–Class II violators. In a six-month period from January 1979, the Columbia office initiated 13 cases with 50 arrests, of which four defendants were Class I violators, three were class II, 16 were Class III, and 27 were class IV. These cases involved marijuana/cocaine major conspiracies and involved the seizure of aircrafts, 33,000 lbs. of marijuana and the formation of Mobile Task Force #326, which implicated public officials in federal, state, and local government and identified the organization known as 'The Company' that had assets of over 25 million dollars.

DEA headquarters analysis showed that 67% of our office cases were DEA-initiated cases with 1.1% of the regional manpower that we contributed 26% of the region's arrest, 1.8% of the region's Class I and II arrests and 8.1% of DEA-initiated investigations. The analysis concluded that arrests per agent exceeded the national average by approximately seven times! Norm and I were honored to receive a quality step increase in recognition of our achievement. This was made possible by our Ad Hoc team effort and was also recognized by the Attorney General of the United States.

We were doing our job as we had planned and were not about to stop. Morale ran high in all agencies involved, and I never saw this much enthusiasm in my years as a law enforcement officer. Of course, as my old boss Tom Cash used to say to me, "Pete, just remember, no good deed goes unpunished." Boy, he was right, and the shit was slowly cooking up and about to hit the fan!

Every boss that I have known always had their own sources of information that were closely kept secret and totally discreet because of their valuable information. Just then Janice came in my office and advised me that someone was here to introduce himself to me. This person was well known in Columbia. She came back escorting the individual who immediately introduced himself. "Mr. Charette, it's finally time for us to meet. Call me Slim," he said smiling.

"Slim, it is from here on. Have a seat. It's a pleasure to meet you. Would you care for some coffee?" Janice walked in with two coffees having already asked if he would like one! I started laughing and said, "Jan, you're the best. Always one step ahead of me!" We all laughed. "Please hold all calls!"

"Done!" she replied as she shut the door.

Slim said, "I have been reading about you almost every day in the newspaper for the past 8 months. I was amazed on your success with our law enforcement agencies and the figures whose asses you have so far put in jail! Quite an accomplishment, Pete. The 'good ole boys' are in total panic mode, especially a lot of the politicians. I never thought I'd see the day when our so-called honest politicians and police agencies' heads would be walking on glass." He paused and laughed!

"Slim. I'm glad to hear that the message is clear, and they're getting a clear message that the good old boy system is being uncovered!"

"Let me ask you straight out! Have you heard the name 'Claire Manors' who runs a Cathouse in Lexington, County?"

"Yes, I have word that some of our targets are clients along with a lot of politicians in this state and cops!"

"You got it! I have been a client myself, and that's confidential information between us, right?"

"Right, what are you proposing?"

"It's simple. She has a townhome for her Cat House, and the layout is, as you walk in there is a couch facing the front door where the client waits for one of the two girls working to be free. The back of the living room has a side bedroom and the same layout on other side. A kitchen is to the left where Claire sits at the kitchen table. She sits with her back to the wall, facing the clients, and there is a small coffee table in front of the couch that has a clear glass salad bowl containing marijuana cigarettes and cocaine for the clients.

"Claire always keeps her large purse open on the table, which contains a .38 cal. pistol loaded for quick access, and her black diary with all the names of her political clients and government officials, senators, both state and federal as well as the names of attorneys and judges, etc. I have seen the book and it's titled Who's Who in South Carolina." Slim stopped and smiled, then finished. "Drug bosses, like Carl Hawkins, Vic Jeffers and many others. This ledger is gold!

"Okay, Slim, why are you doing this? I want the truth. Don't Jack me around because you will lose and regret it! Trust me, I play a serious game and believe in putting these pieces of shit in prison!! I have no use for crooked politicians and cops! Are we clear?"

"Yes! Perfectly clear. That's why I am here for the same reason you have!"

"Great! I will get with the team and plan a takedown and seize the book! All I want you to do is to go in as a regular and when you come out, signal by taking off your hat which will mean that dope is in plain view and it's good to go! Leave and we will hit five minutes after you."

"Sounds good. Friday at 9:00 p.m. sharp! I'll arrive and go in! Looking forward to working with you! See you next Monday at 10:30 a.m." They then shook hands.

"You got it, Pete! Stay safe."

I went to Norm's office, and he looked up and said, "What's up?"

"Norm! I just met with Slim my CI who advised me about a Claire Manors, a Madame in Lexington County, who is operating a whore house and entertaining her clients with cocaine/ marijuana while they wait to be serviced by her two girls in this townhouse complex. Does this name mean anything to you?"

"Oh, Hell yeah! I have been told by SLED, Lexington County Sheriff's NARCS, that her clientele consists of the who's who in local/state politicians, federal politicians, drug traffickers, and some law enforcement officials. The team has been trying to find sources to take us in! No one has come forward so far for fear of their life!"

"Guess what? We are in this coming Friday with SLIM who will go in and come out and give the signal if dope is on the coffee table in front of clients sitting on the living room couch waiting to be relieved of their desires that they can't get at home!"

"Pete, you made my day! Yes! Warning! Get ready for all hell to break once the headlines are on the front page of the Record! Our phone will be ringing all day. I expect it will and the reason is to get to her source of supply and identify who's dirty in politics and hopefully see who we can trust and not trust in our job and to put the big fish on alert that we are coming after them, regardless of their title and position.

"Call the team and have them come here in an hour! Don't give a reason, just advise them it's mandatory attendance!"

"Yes! Sir," I answered. "I'll be in my office. I got to make some calls to Miami, Atlanta, and tell Sonny Clark and Buford and MacNelly that I want them here also."

"Got it." Laughing, he said, "You're going to need a bodyguard after this goes down."

I responded, "No problem. I got the perfect guy in my mind for that task!"

"Oh shit! The snake! It's good we think alike!" Norm added.

As I left and stopped at Janice's desk, I reached for my wallet and took out $40 after which she immediately said, "Yes, Boss! I will get 15 coffees and creams. Just your look and Norm's bouncing around like a bunch of Kangaroos tells me something big is about ready to explode!"

"Now how in the hell did you know that?

"It isn't hard to see your two fools' looks, when something big is about to happen."

"Okay! I want you in at this meeting and take your shorthand notes for the file name Claire Lee Manors et.al."

"For real? See I knew you would act like a fool also! Got you!"

We borrowed some chairs from our insurance company friends next door, and at 3:00 p.m. all were present with curious looks.

"Okay! Pete everyone is here, and I'm getting out of town before this place blows up! See you guys." He waived as Norm started to leave.

"Stop! You coward. Shut the front door, lock it, and get back here quick." Everyone began to laugh. "Anyone who has handcuffs, please put them on him!" By now, everyone was in stitches.

The Snake said, "Shit! We're all going to jail, aren't we?"

"Okay! I hate to call this meeting on short notice, guys. Like my Mentor used to tell me 'The one thing that you will learn about this job is you will never know what will happen.'"

Almost everyone nodded with a "Yep."

"Does the name Clair Manors mean anything to anyone?"

The responses varied from "Oh shit" to "Damn" along with laughs and snickers.

I briefed them all and told them that we will strike at 9 p.m. at her Lexington town home. "Because of her fame and her Who's Who in South Carolina clients, this investigation is to be held totally secret from heads of departments! I assure you that your chiefs are not mentioned in her famous black book in her purse along with her .38 Caliber S&W. I will take all the heat and that each one of you be sworn to secrecy." Everyone welcomed this investigation with joy. It was long overdue.

"I want you all to know that you and we are the only ones that will know what we discover along with the state attorney of Lexington County who will prosecute this case. The diary will be held in evidence in my safe, per instruction of The Attorney General of the Department of Justice. Please, if you get calls on this matter, please keep a log, with date/time received and name and phone number. The reason for not notifying your department heads if asked is that we do not want them to be accused of leaking this raid. I am here to protect the people who have entrusted us to serve and protect them no matter where our investigations take us. Thank God that we all work alike, and we have a binding trust.

"Okay! Any questions? Norm will be in charge and, Sonny, it's your case for prosecution. I will be there with all of you! Just remember this. Once the source comes out and lifts his cap, that's the signal to move in. Claire will be sitting at the kitchen table and immediately grab her handbag and give it to me. We will be on location at 8:00 p.m. Okay! Norm the floor is all yours." We terminated our raid meeting and were all on location on time. The Confidential Informant arrived at 8:05 p.m.

At 9:00 p.m. the CI came out and took his cap off and readjusted it then got into his vehicle and left the complex. The raid team entered the townhouse, the door already unlocked, and within 4 minutes the residence was secured. I witnessed two males sitting on the living room couch and placed under arrest by Deputy Tim Crocker. On the table was a bowl containing suspected marijuana. Sitting behind the kitchen table, facing the living room was

Claire Manors being detained by Sgt. Sonny Clark. He handed me Claire's purse.

Claire said, "Mr. Charette, please don't take my address book." I opened her purse which had a gun and took out the address book advising her that it was part of our investigation and would be locked in a safe at my office. A quick glance at the address /phone book, answered my question as to why she did not want this book out of her possession. Seeing some of the names immediately substantiated what we were told about well-known politicians, etc.

Ms. Manors was charged with operating a house of prostitution, possession of marijuana with intent to distribute, and possession and operating gambling devices. Her associate was charged with prostitution and possession of marijuana with intent to distribute.

The raid on the house of prostitution proved to be extremely successful by all and created a scandalous investigation. When I arrived at the office the next morning, the phone lines were going crazy.

Janice immediately advised me that the U.S. Attorney Tom Lydon had come to our office and demanded to be given Ms. Manors Diary/Phone Book. I told him that I was ordered that no one was authorized to take or see the book by order of the Attorney General of the United States. This did not sit well with him at all, and he came to see me and demanded to have access to the book. I told him that I had my orders from Washington and could not give him access, and he needed to discuss this with the AG himself. He turned red faced and stormed out of my office.

I immediately called my superiors and referred this matter to them. The next phone call I received came from a U.S. politician from Washington who demanded to have a meeting with me because he had been contacted by the media who alleged that his name was mentioned in this book and wanted to meet with me in person to resolve this issue. I advised him that the AG had instructed that no one was to have access to this book.

He insinuated that I had to grant him an immediate meeting. I responded very kindly and politely by saying, "Senator, I'm sorry, but you will have to take your place in line like others who have called. Have great day, Sir!" Then I hung up.

As I did, I knew that I would be getting a phone call from DEA HQ! Sure, enough, the Director called and said the congressman called to voice his displeasure of my telling him to "take his place in line with the others!" I confirmed this and advised the boss, that no one who inquired about the book could be given access and the AG was referring the case to the FBI to investigate this matter. My boss concurred and thanked me for this and passed it on to the group "Great job!"

We were inundated with calls all day about Ms. Manors' arrest. I knew that this was going to shake a lot of people and that we needed to be aware of our surroundings. I got a call from several assistant U.S. attorneys who congratulated us for making this case and that the U.S. attorney was beside himself and expressed his feelings about me in a very descriptive way! They also told me to be careful because the "Good Old Boys" will be meeting about your shaking up corruption in this state. This made us feel proud that we were making an impact and would not stop doing our job as required.

Everyone was briefed and told to be on guard. "We have a bull's eyes on us so report any intelligence on this to your boss, Norm, and me."

I received more phone calls from law enforcement chiefs and judges warning me to be cautious because word on the street was that our Informal Task Force was out to get crooked politicians who had ties with drug traffickers in the State of South Carolina.

Not too long after these warnings, things started to happen, proving that the warnings were a reality. My experience with corruption began early in my career and made me determine that law enforcement had an obligation to prevent it from becoming a cancer in our profession. My first shift commander with the

Broward County Sheriff's Department was my first arrest, and I learned early that these corrupt individuals deserved to be put in jail.

Due to the increase in cases and activities in our enforcement efforts, Norm, Janice and I had a meeting during which we decided that there were no questions in our mind that we needed additional people to keep up with the case load. Word traveled fast in government agencies while I travelled to Miami to have a sit down with Dave Connelly and John Van Diver to make my case. As usual my request was met with enthusiasm and from both. I couldn't ask for better bosses than these two great friends. I had a friend in the Miami office named Charles Shaming who had asked me if there was any way of getting him transferred to our office. Chuck was assisting the U.S. Attorney's Office in South Carolina with a corruption case involving unfortunately corrupt SLED narcotic agents. Chuck was a survivor of the BNDD building crash in Miami. I told him that I would be honored to have him once we got the okay to get additional agents.

Approval from Washington was granted for two agent positions and one additional secretary. I made it known to Dave Connelly that I wanted Chuck while the other position could be selected through the Vacancy Announcement process. This position was filled by Agent Anthony Duarte who was a great agent and was immediately accepted by all. Chuck was an expert in putting together conspiracy cases and was fantastic in assisting agents with these types of cases.

5
The Company

Our office was growing, and cases were constantly being made with our informal task force. Charles finally had reported for work and was a great addition to our team.

Norm came in and advised me that SLED informed him that they needed to work a sensitive case with us on an international marijuana smuggling ring based in St. Louis and were going to use the Darlington Racetrack Airport to bring in one plane loaded with 1,300 lbs. of marijuana. He advised me that this organization had bribed a SLED Investigator with $8,350 to be a lookout for them when the planes would be coming in to offload the drug to trucks that would then transport the marijuana to St. Louis.

"The surprise was that the current Chairman of the Democratic Party of South Carolina, a lawyer who recruited the SLED Agent Billy Mozingo was a great friend of his."

"Norm, what was his role going to be for them?" I asked.

"Pete, I met with him, Steve Smith, and Lt. Mabrey and he advised that the lawyer John R. Etheridge needed him to be at the airport when the plane came in and to monitor SLED/ DEA police radio to ensure that there was no activity by them in the area. The offloading of the 1300 lbs. would be done by the St. Louis group consisting of 14 individuals on January 24. They had several vans and trucks ready for the offload.

"Sweet Jesus, Norm! This is highly sensitive, and we will take this group down hard and fast!"

"Pete! One other thing you need to know is that our U.S. Attorney Tom Lydon (deceased) is a close friend of Etheridge who is being named a Federal Judge by the Carter Administration."

"Norm! Starting now not one word to anyone outside our office, and I will communicate this immediately to SAIC John Vandiver in Miami and the SAIC in Atlanta. This will result in having the Attorney General get involved for sure."

Once the briefing occurred with the bosses, The AG ordered that no contact with the U.S. Attorney be made on this case and that he would be informed of any action occurring on this daily. We also received word from SLED that the arrival of the plane would be on January 24 at the Gedra Air Service Field near Dawesville, SC.

A meeting was held on the 23rd with SLED and our team and everyone was assigned arrest duties which consisted of seizing the marijuana shipment, plane, cars, trucks, radio equipment and van utilized by Dugan, a paraplegic who oversaw communication to the plane etc.

Norm had also secured with SLED a Search Warrant for Etheridge's office.

In the early morning hours, the arrest team positioned themselves at the Darlington Racetrack and waited for the signal from Agent Mozingo to move in for the arrest! He kept us appraised of what was occurring at the air service with the suspects.

Finally, Mozingo advised that the plane was coming in on its final approach for landing. We could hear the twin engine plane motors and awaited to move in once the trucks approached the plane to start offloading the bails of marijuana.

Within five minutes the green light was given to move in. Approximately 10 police cars came onto the field and surrounded the plane and trucks and arrested everyone in perfect swift surprising action. Everyone was on the ground being handcuffed and being processed on paper for court appearance.

During this processing, SLED Agent Murry Fant called me and advised me that Mr. Dugan refused to give any information. He sat on his wheelchair, looking extremely agitated toward Murry and me. I walked up to him with Murry and identified myself and told him, "Sir, you're under federal arrest and we need your name, date of birth, address, weight and height to process you with the U.S. Magistrate! Now! What is your name?"

His response was, "F. U.! Murray, put FU for the name on the form!"

"What is your DOB, weight, height, etc.?

His response was FU, and for height he became very irritated and stood up pulling himself up by the arm handles. Based on my visual observation, I told Murray for height put down 3 feet approximately. At that point he became enraged and called me vile words. With a smile to Murray, I said, "He's all yours!" Then told Dugan, "See you in court."

Norm had taken some prisoners to the Sheriff's Department and was going with Steve Smith to serve the search warrant at Mr. Etheridge's office when suddenly who was walking into the booking desk area but Mr. Etheridge and his attorney who notified Norm that Mr. Etheridge had received a phone call from Mr. Lydon that he was going to be arrested by SLED/DEA.

Norm immediately called me and advised me that Mr. Lydon had called Etheridge and warned him of the upcoming arrest. This phone call consequently impeded our ability to find any evidence we sought.

I immediately called our secretary, and asked Janice if Lydon had called! She answered, "Yes! He was hot and wants you to call him immediately!" She continued by saying she had just hung up with the DEA office secretary in Charleston, SC who called to inquire if Johnny Etheridge had been arrested and that they heard our office had arrested him. Now we understood what had most likely occurred.

I immediately called the bosses and received a response that the AG Griffin Bell wanted me to call Mr. Lydon and advise him that I would be at his office in an hour, and to make sure to immediately advise him of his rights and for him to call the AG ASAP.

I called Mr. Lydon who immediately started admonishing me on the phone. I simply said, "Stop. I am on my way to see you." Then I hung up.

Norm, Chuck, and I left Darlington and headed back to the Federal Courthouse to meet with Mr. Lydon. As we arrived, we noticed that the Assistant U.S. Attorney was on the courthouse steps waiting for us. As we approached him, he said, "Pete, Norm, what in the hell is going on? Lydon is flaming red and out to get you, Pete!"

Smiling, I said, "Calm down. You're going to have a breakdown. I apologize for circumventing Investigative Protocol but was instructed by the AG not to say anything until the case was completed; we were sworn to secrecy. Just come in with us and watch and listen. It will be short and sweet!"

We entered the U.S. Attorney's office and the secretary said, "Go on in. He's waiting!" We entered and shut the door.

"Mr. Charette! You better have a reason for not advising us of this case," he hurled in a loud tone! I could tell that he was not a happy man at this point, and his face was blood red with anger!

"I have an answer for our actions, I have been directed by the Attorney General of the United States to tell you this," and turning to Chuck Shaming, continued. "Please advise Mr. Lydon of his rights since he is under investigation by the A.G. I was to ensure that this was done in front of witnesses. Chuck, go ahead!"

Chuck had not been prepared for this and rightfully appeared slightly shocked, having to do this. He read him his rights, and I immediately thanked him for seeing us after which the three of us left.

Upon going upstairs to our office, Norm kept saying, "Damn it's over for us!"

Responding, I said, "Great job, guys! We have more work to do. Norm, call Saint Louis and brief them!"

"Roger that!"

The Department of Justice initiated an FBI investigation into certain allegations concerning public officials in South Carolina. The U.S. Attorney Tom Lydon went out of town for a week.

Summary of this Corrupt Smuggling Investigation

This investigation took more than 6 months in Darlington County, South Carolina and ended up being one of the largest smuggling marijuana operations in the U.S. ever solved.

The coordinated investigation involved five states as well as Colombia and South America. Marijuana seized had a street value of more than $900,000.

The St. Louis Indictment of "The Company" eventually charged nearly 70 persons, quashing a highly organized marijuana ring. It had been described as one of the largest marijuana operations in the country. The indictment was a 45 count.

The Company smuggled more than 150 tons to three states. The street value was $120 million, and seized in a three-year period were 78,000 pounds.

(Note: UPI Archives12/13/80 by Tim Bryant)

This investigation is further proof that good liaison and team effort leads to great achievement in destroying drug smuggling organizations and identifying corruption by politicians.

6
Death Threats

After the arrest of members of the "The Company" along with a political democratic chairman of South Carolina, I started getting phone calls from various honest politicians and police chiefs, attorneys, judges as well as federal, state and local law enforcement friends that the word was out that my name was being tossed around by these suspected corrupt individuals that I needed to be removed permanently!"

When this happened, we had to immediately take these threats seriously and not disregard them. Even today, alleged threats are real and need to be reported to our department heads with corroborated proof. I immediately reported this information to our team and agency.

I could continue with hundreds of cases made in 4 years which shook the criminal underworld in South Carolina, but something happened that brought everything to a halt for me and required me to be transferred to Atlanta as the Supervisor of Enforcement for DEA.

I received a phone call at my residence from the wife of the Solicitor of Richland County, SC, Jim Anders (deceased) who was a good friend and one of the best in South Carolina. She was almost hysteric but forced the words out. "Pete, you need to come right away at the house, Jim is in a panic mode and asked me to call you to come right way, please hurry!"

"I'm on my way. Be there in 45 minutes. Lock your door!" I

immediately called Norm and told him to get dressed. I would be picking him up in 15 minutes and hung up!

I drove to his house at 2 a.m. with blue light flashing. Norm was waiting outside, and I briefed him on the phone conversation.

Norm said, "What the hell is going on, Pete?"

"Norm, I'm guessing it has to do with this threat on me! If it is, the shit will hit the fan, big time."

We pulled up in the driveway and Mrs. Anders was waiting with door opened! "Go to the kitchen. He's sitting at the table. I got coffee for both of you!"

"Jim! What's going on?" I shook his hand that was trembling.

Jim said" Pete! They're going to kill you! This is crazy!" He was shaking his head from one side to the other! "My God, they are crazy!"

"Relax," I replied staring down at Norm.

Norm was wearing a stunned look and said, "What the hell?"

"Jim, calm down and take some deep breaths, slow down, and tell me from the start where you were? And who said this?"

Jim started to compose himself and apologized for his display of fear. He then began. "After work, I went to our Good Old Boy politician bar near the Capitol on Main St. where we all meet for a few beers before we go home. This is how we catch up with all the political news of the day!

"One of the men at the table waived at me to come and sit with a couple senators and two criminal attorneys. I sat down, and everybody greeted me then we started to talk about local politics for a while when one of the senators said, 'Jim, what do you think of this DEA guy Pete Charette who is creating havoc in the state, arresting politicians and sheriffs, police chiefs, and SLED Agents?'

"Everybody was looking at me with a straight face for an answer, and I answered, "He's doing a great job, and finally we got somebody that's got balls to put corrupted individuals in jail!

"The senator responded by saying, 'Jim, he's getting too close to the top and we need to take him out, and his family too. Are you in with us on this?'

"I jumped up out of my seat! I asked them if they were crazy, that this was a conspiracy against a federal agent! I told them that I was out of here, and I couldn't believe that they wanted to do this! I stormed out of the bar and went home and had my wife call you to come here. Pete, the guy heading this meeting was a senior senator!"

(Note: Mr. Anders information was corroborated and proved he was telling the truth.)

Norm and I left the residence, and we discussed this at length then briefed our team at the office. Everyone agreed that we needed to be aware of our surroundings and check our vehicles for any tampering, etc.

I communicated this information to the DEA and FBI. The FBI came and met with Norm and me, and subsequently we stayed out of this investigation. This was serious and needed to be reported immediately to the BNDD director and my boss immediately.

Everybody at the office was briefed and told to be cautious when working.

I left the office for home and drove around for an hour to check to see if I was being followed by anyone, using evasive detection procedures. I intentionally did not say anything to my wife in order not to cause her to fear and panic. I had my own plan in my mind how to put an end to this as soon as possible. Threats were sometime part of the job and accepted, but these SOBS crossed the line by including my family in this threat!

I awakened at 2 a.m. to grab my gun and check the house out for anything suspicious. Everything was fine as I was looking out the dining room window which faced the street for any parked suspicious vehicles. Approximately three houses up, a vehicle was parked on the street, and I could see a dark shadow of a person in the driver's seat. Okay! You want to play game on! I thought.

I got dressed, slipped out through the back patio sliding door, cut through the backyard of our neighbor's property onto the street and headed up five houses. From there I cut through the owner's yard, crossed the street then worked through the neighbor's front yard and crawled low toward the car. I could see smoke rising out of the driver's car window.

It was time to make a formal introduction to this POS. Quickly I drove the barrel of my Walter PPKS 9 mm, to the neck of this driver saying, "Move and I will blow your head off you mother f...."

"Pete! It's me... Snake!"

"Snake! I Could have blown you away, you crazy SOB!" I let out a laugh of relief which shook my head and relaxed my body. "What the hell are doing here? It's almost 3 a.m."

"Pete, you're my friend, and I'll be dammed if the POS will get to you and your family! I got my AR-15 and served in Vietnam. I know how to deal with these guys."

"Snake, thank you, my friend. We need to talk, and no one is to know about tonight! "Boss, I agree. Let's go to the Pancake House and decide how we should handle this."

Word somehow had gotten out to law enforcement. We kept alert and work went on!

A week later, we were informed that there was talk by some politicians, that an unnamed senator was paid a visit at night by an unknown person and was informed that if anything happened to Mr. Charette, along with his family, that the senator's family would be dealt with, and he would disappear very quickly and never be heard from again. This was confirmed by Mr. Anders who received a call from a friend, that the contract was dismissed immediately against me and my family.

Going through my mail I read the monthly government OPM Bulletin and learned of a change of Supervisor's grade rating. The new definition of a supervisor was that "Anyone who supervises and manages one or more employees in any office, is to be promoted to a grade GS- 14." This new policy was placed in effect one month prior to reading this. This update was never communicated to us at Grade 13. I immediately called the Miami Administrative Officer who told me he was aware of this and that I should not pursue this matter. I immediately thanked him and hung up. I did not accept his advice, so I called my ASAIC and advised him of my concern. He was hot and told me he would immediately check this out and call me back. Within one hour Dave called me and advised me that The SAIC called Washington Headquarters. And they assured him that this would be immediately implemented. I was extremely pleased of that news along with my friends who were promoted.

The four years in Colombia, SC was the most rewarding assignment I ever had with this great team. I received word that I was being transferred to the Atlanta office as Group Supervisor. I was honored by a fabulous going away banquet, which was attended by chiefs of police, state agents, U.S. attorneys, and SLED officials and agents. All attendees to this day remain great friends. Unfortunately, some have passed away and are missed by all of us. May they rest in peace. (Norm Shumate, Lt. Laurence McNeely, Janice Goggans Charette, and Dennis "Snake" Craig. They were the best of the best!

I'm proud to say that I was able to have BNDD hire the following team members as agents who all excelled in their new careers and are still close friends. James Matthews became one of BNDD's agents and worked in Miami, Thailand, and retired as a supervisor.

He retired and became sheriff of Kershaw County, SC. Robert Cathey worked for the SC Tax Bureau and after our meeting, he expressed a desire to work for BNDD. Since the BNDD was just starting the Asset Forfeiture Seizure Program, I called Washington and got him hired. He became a great asset to BNDD. He made several historic cases, especially when assigned as an agent in Charleston, SC and broke our record there for the largest marijuana seizure (110,000 pounds) while working undercover. He retired as a supervisor in Seattle of the Asset Removal Group.

Billy Watson and Chuck Gardner all retired as supervisors. Chuck Shaming retired as the Special Agent in Charge of DEA, In Columbia, SC.

One of the most special occurrences while working in South Carolina was the birth of my second daughter Celine, born on May 5, 1977. I went to the hospital to be there for her birth. As I entered through the emergency room, my eyes wandered to a bearded doctor wearing a white smock and a stethoscope around his neck and a writing tablet in his hands. I immediately recognized this crazy man to be "The Snake." I walked over and said, "Snake, what in the hell are you up too?"

He quietly responded, "I'm working undercover on a hospital pharmacist who is dealing drugs."

"I'm out of here see you at the office."

Dennis "THE SNAKE" was also known as the man with many faces and disguises. He had put me in an awkward position, testifying in Magistrate Court, when testifying on arrest facts with members of the company's bond hearing.

I was being crossed examined by a defense attorney and asked, "Mr. Charette can you please tell the court who was the priest that arrested my client?"

"Sir, there was no priest at the crime scene!"

Mr. Charette, are you aware of the statute on committing perjury under oath?"

"Yes, I am, and there was no priest on the arrest team, sir!"

"Your Honor, I wish to put this man on notice of committing perjury under oath."

Judge Cantrell immediately called for a recess and for me, the Assistant U.S. Attorney, and defense lawyer to his chambers. Judge Gambrell advised me, "Pete, this is a serious allegation. Are you sure there was no priest there?"

"Your Honor, I am 100% sure!"

"Okay! Let's go back into court and the defense can ask one more time and, Pete, clear your mind before you answer the question."

Returning on the stand, I looked around and noticed our team members there looking perplexed. In the back row of the courtroom, looking at me with a smile was the Snake. I immediately said to myself, SHIT! Dennis.

I immediately turned to the judge and said, "Your Honor, I must apologize to the court. There was an agent dressed in a priest's robe and white collar who was first on the scene and arrested this man, pointing to the defendant. Looking around the courtroom and seeing him, immediately reminded me that Agent Craig wore a fake identity costume to avoid suspicion while surveilling the ongoing movements of any suspects doing countersurveillance, looking for police."

Judge Futch was trying to hold back from laughing and the courtroom exploded in laughter. I looked at Dennis and couldn't help myself to laugh also.

Judge Gambrel said he was glad to hear this and continued with the hearing.

Dennis bought drinks for his "penance"! (R.I.P. Dennis, you were the best.)

Now a new challenge was ahead with unbelievable agents and cases that became historic in the history of this country. On to Atlanta!

7
Group Supervisor, Atlanta, Georgia

I reported to work and met with the ASAIC Buzz Durrell who was my boss when I was in South Carolina. He was very pleased to have me now in Atlanta as the new supervisor. We discussed numerous details of my enforcement group and met with the boss Ray Vinsick (deceased). Both emphasized that they would support me 100% as the GS (Group Supervisor).

I advised them that I appreciated their support, and that I was ready to make cases.

Buzz took me to the group office where all the agents were waiting for my arrival. Buzz said, "Well, you all have been waiting for this guy, who you all know! So, Pete, you're on your own,

"Thanks Buzz! I'm glad to be here. I'm going to make this short and to the point. Patty would please take notes for this meeting?"

"Yes sir!

"The first thing is that I know you have been wondering why are you here? I have nothing to hide and will always be up front with you. I am part of this team, and you all know me. I am always open and that's my style of management. So I was shocked when I got appointed to this position to say the least! Because of events by a group of politicians making a contract to kill me and my family, which came to my attention and was cancelled swiftly after the leader of this plot had a midnight visit by a masked individual who delivered a message to him stating 'Cancel this plot within the next 24 hours on Mr. Charette and his family. If not, you will suffer along with your family a very swift disappearance from this state, never to be seen again!

"I received a call that day from the Solicitor of Richland County Jim Anders that rumors at the state Capitol were passed on to him, that the contract was cancelled, and this Senator left town on a family vacation!

"Now I was informed that someone had filed a complaint that there were numerous incidents of alcohol abuse by some agents at the DEA office, and my name came up to be assigned as a supervisor since threats were being directed at me. So here I am and ready to work with you in making cases!

"My agenda is to ensure that we make big cases and that all of you are responsible to initiate them. Looking at the case log, I notice that some make cases and others simply assist. I expect starting today that everyone is required to make cases.

"I know that some of you have been here for years, and my office door is always open should anyone feel that a change would be good for you." As suspected, a few agents came to my office, expressing their wishes to be re-assigned to new offices since they had been here for over 5 years and desired a change. I accepted their request and arrangement were made to re- locate them within 90 days.

I individually met with all agents and discussed with them what their goals were and assured them that they had my full support in making sure that they achieve their goals.

I made it clear to all that I was asked to accept this position due to complaints by someone that there were numerous occurrences when some agents were involved in consumption of alcohol while on duty and observed returning to the office intoxicated. I reiterated to them that when on the job, there was no excuse for this type of behavior and that this type of conduct should stop immediately. I'm a firm believer that anyone who allows this to occur deserves to be removed immediately. I finished by assuring them that I was here to work with them on making this office number one in our division. I also advised them that we work as a team.

"It's time for lunch and please be back by 2 p.m. where I will individually meet with each one of you in private.

The Atlanta office at that time only had one Enforcement Group consisting of 15 agents and one secretary. The rest of the office consisted of an Intelligence Group, Diversion Group, Training Officer, a SAIC, ASAIC, File Clerk, Administrative Officer, and 5 Secretaries. The Atlanta Office also had seven District DEA offices in Georgia, South Carolina, North Carolina, and Tennessee.

I then met with the U.S. Attorney Mr. Larry Thompson, who later became Deputy Attorney of the United States, and his staff of Assistant U.S. Attorneys, who were highly respected by us. All complimented DEA for their professionalism and case making. I assured them of my full support.

I also met with the U.S. Custom Department heads, Atlanta Police Chief and Narcotic Bureau group where I had one agent assigned to that office, the Georgia Bureau of Investigation Director and Narcotic Chief, where we had two agents assigned, and the head of the Federal Organized Crime Chief and supervisor, for whom my wife worked as secretary to this unit. I also met with the Cobb County Sheriff Bill Hudson, who was a great friend and had the best aggressive Narcotic Bureau in the State of Georgia. His Sgt. of Narcotic was and still is a great friend, Jimmy Maxwell. His unit worked with us daily, and some of their detectives became DEA agents in later years. At that time, we had great liaison with the FBI, but they did not work narcotic cases and referred those to us and assisted us on these cases.

Approximately 8 months later, the FBI received authority to work on Narcotic Cases and had to be trained for two weeks by our DEA Training Officer, and me, in Tennessee, Georgia and South Carolina. Within a 6 months' period, significant cases started to increase, and morale was extremely good, with some exceptions which I will discuss later.

I will only list some of the major cases that were extremely significant and most famous in the history of drug investigations in the United States. Some involved corruption by sheriffs, politicians, and the Mafia. I must admit that after a month of ensuring that the entire team would work together by assisting each other, the case production increased by 75% and morale was at a high.

Unfortunately, there was an attempt to bring down the existing group, by a handful of disgruntled employees who attempted to create racial discrimination toward agents of all races. This was reported to me by agents who were new to the group and wanted no part in this.

Upon learning of this, I immediately advised the SAIC at lunch. He was told that a secret meeting had been called on a Friday after work hours where the head of this attempted coup ordered the agents and selected staff to stay behind at the end of the day, to be briefed on this matter.

Those who opposed were warned that they were new hires and still on probation and would be dismissed if they didn't go along with this plan. They had identified for me those agents who were leading this attempted coup.

I was shocked along with the SAIC Ray Vinsick and the training officer Gerry Miller. Present also were the two agents who furnished this info to me. They were advised to go about their work and praised for bringing this shocking information to us. Those agents ended up having an outstanding and distinguished career.

I advised the SAIC, that we needed to inform HQ Internal Affair of this and request an immediate investigation by them immediately. Also disclosed to us was that the head of this coup had illegally purchased new tires for his car because he did not like the ones he had and gave them to the tire company employee's mechanic. This information was given to me by someone who got this firsthand from the tire dealership.

Within 24 hours, an Internal Affair team, came to the office and asked that an entire office meeting of all agents and staff be held in the conference room. The SAIC, ASAIC, and I were asked not to sit in on this meeting. We learned that there was a lot of anger at the meeting once this was disclosed and several agents were identified by fellow agents and were requested to leave the meeting. This was granted.

Internal affair inspector also asked to interview the individual at the tire dealership which was immediately done. He corroborated the information and showed the tires that were given to him and were on his car.

This matter was swiftly handled by DEA, and those who were responsible for this horrible and disgraceful attempted coup! All parties involved were transferred to different offices within a few months of this shameless act.

Finally, things got back to normal, and morale remained high.

Corruption Cases — Sheriff Jimmy Glass et. al, 11-03-1981
Charges:
1. Conspiring to import cocaine and Methaqualone into the United States (One Count)
2. Conspiring to obstruct, delay, and affect commerce through the means of extortion (Two Counts)
3. Importing methaqualone (One Count)

Arrested:
1. Sheriff Jimmy Glass, Henry County, GA.
   (Guilty: 35-year sentence)
2. Henry County Probate Judge, Larry Tew
   (Guilty: 30-year sentence)
3. Henry County Chief of Police Herschel Childs
   (Guilty: 30-year sentence)
4. Berry Hill Airport Manager William H. Hinton

(Guilty: 30-year sentence)
5. Eddie F. Black (Guilty: 30-year sentence)
6. John Hathorn (Guilty: 30-year sentence)

This investigation began when I received a phone call from an ex- drug trafficker pilot, who introduced himself as a Canadian and had read about me in the newspaper. He advised me that he would like to meet with me since he had stopped flying drugs into the U.S. He advised me that the Sheriff of Henry County Jimmy Glass protected him from arrest whenever he flew into the Berry Hill Airport and paid the sheriff and his co-conspirators each time.

I asked for him to come to my office where we could further discuss this in person, and he agreed too.

I immediately asked Agent Larry Sproat to come to my office. "Larry, shut the door. Looks like we are possibly arresting some politician!"

"Sounds good to me, Pete!"

"Larry, tell me what you know about Sheriff Jimmy Glass of Henry County?"

"God almighty, Pete, he's the most powerful Sheriff in Georgia," "He answered with a surprised and excited look.

"Great, Larry, you and I are going to meet a source that is out of the drug business as a pilot, who flew drug loads into Berry Hill Airport and paid the sheriff, county judge, chief of police and airport manager for clearance and Police protection for escort of the drugs.

I'm assigning you this case so pick your team because we are going to have this pilot call the sheriff and tell him that he's back in business and wants protection to bring cocaine / methaqualone into the airport, like old times and need police escort to Atlanta.

Larry "God, Pete, this is big!

"Wacker, (Larry's nickname) we got to keep this very quiet between us and the team! Nothing to others in this group or office! I've learned from real experience, 'Loose lips sink ship!'"

"Frog," (which was my nickname by him and the group) Larry said laughing, "You got it!"

The meeting went extremely well, and this source made a recorded call, advising to the Sheriff who gave a green light to fly in. Larry got his team who were the best in the office together. I appointed him the case agent since he had extensive experience as an Atlanta narcotics detective and was the best agent the Atlanta Police Department had. The team members consisted of Agents Gene Bachman, Don Augustine, Chuck Crane, Pilot Charlie Overstreet, FBI Agent Rick Dean, FBI Supervisor (Name withheld). Also present at the arrest at the Holiday Inn Motel, in Cobb County, was Asst. US Attorney Craig Gillen.

Judge Tew requested Undercover Agent Larry Sproat to fly into Berry Hill Airport with the pilot for a meeting. Sproat and Pilot arrived on November 1 and were greeted by Judge TEW, Chief Glass and Airport Manager Hinton. Tew advised Larry and Charlie that they needed to check the plane inside and out to make sure there was no hidden camera and microphone. They conducted a thorough search and were satisfied. TEW also wrote on a piece of paper the plane's N Number (Airplane Tail Number) to verify that it was not a police aircraft. Once this was done, Tew instructed Sproat to come in three days prior to Stockbridge, Georgia and get a motel room, and for the plane to fly the load of cocaine/ methaqualone in on November 3, 1981. Everyone left and the area. Larry planned to fly the drugs in cardboard boxes. The fake drugs were nothing but plastic bags of baking flour. Tew also instructed Larry to make sure he had the $30,000 money bag with him at the motel.

After the arrest, Tew who cooperated at trial, testified that when the sheriff originally discussed this profitable plan to provide protection to drug smugglers, that he knew that some sheriffs in Georgia were getting $50, 000 per load, and that this should be what they get for this load! When this was discussed, Larry and our Pilot, stuck to $30,000.

On November 1, Larry checked in to a motel in Stockbridge, registering under the first name of Sonny. He arrived with a van to transport the load from the plane.

On his second day after coming back to the motel from having dinner, Larry walked to his room, heard his undercover's first name being called out "Sonny! Sonny!" Turning around to his surprise was Judge Tew, with two muscular men, saying "We need to talk, NOW!"

Sonny replied "What's Up? "

Tew continued, "Not here in your room!" Once in the room, Tew said, "We need to search you and your room. We don't plan on being caught. We plan on making millions, that's all.

Larry agreed and the two goons patted down his body and checked under carpets, under the bed to ensures his room was not bugged and that he was not a Federal Agent. Everything went smoothly. Tew, thanked him and said, "See you tomorrow at the airport as planned.

Some may ask, "Why was he not surveilled by the team?" Every case is different. This case involved corrupt police officials and politicians. A good undercover agent always assesses who he is dealing with, past records of the "Suspect" if any. He also selects when and where meetings take place. Never let the bad guys choose the rendezvous' location. If for some reason your instinct tells you about These smells for God's sake! Follow your instinct and call the whole thing off! This call is the undercover agent's call, not the supervisor or other senior bosses. I know this for a fact. A friend of mine who was a great DEA undercover agent was killed by some mob hitmen in New York. He had a bad feeling about the people he was supposed to meet and did not want to proceed. But he was ordered to do it by his superiors and consequently did so. In proceeding against his instinct, he was shot and killed.

On November 3, 1981, the plane arrived from the Bahamas

at the airport. After landing, the plane taxied to the terminal. Awaiting was Larry with his van, and as soon as the doors were opened, Larry and Charlie transferred the boxes into the van. Observing was Judge Tew, Chief Childs dressed in his uniform with his police car ready to escort Larry with the van to Atlanta.

Larry immediately departed for Atlanta driving the van escorted by the chief of police.

Larry who had arranged with the team to surveil the parking lot, had gotten two adjoining rooms, one for the UC pay off, the other was for monitoring the bugged undercover room which had been bugged by two FBI tech agents. Present besides me were FBI Supervisor Rick Dean and Assistant US Attorney Mr. Craig Gillen who in my opinion was the best AUSA that I had worked with in Atlanta. Craig had prepared Cooperation documents to offer to these defendants to be arrested.

Tew, Glass and pilot Overstreet came upstairs and entered the room. Glass looked around and then stationed himself outside on the balcony, watching the parking lot for police surveillance activity. Larry arrived and had the money suitcase. He told Tew to sit down at the desk and opened the suitcase. Then he told Tew, "Go ahead and count it!"

After Tew finished counting, he said, "Great it's all there!"

Once this response was heard, FBI Agent Rick Dean followed by two other agents and I opened the adjoining door, guns drawn, and Larry's gun drawn said, "Federal Agents!

You're under arrest!" Judge and Chief Shields were arrested and brought inside the room. Defendants were advised of their rights, and Larry introduced Craig Gillen who advised them that if they wish to assist themselves by cooperating with us, he has documents for them to read and sign. Both agreed without hesitation. Once this was done, Chief Shields and Tew agreed to place a recorded phone call to Sheriff Glass and Bill Hinton.

Sheriff Glass was arrested by DEA and FBI agents at his

residence. Everyone else was arrested and Sheriff Glass was the only one who pleaded not guilty.

During this trial, Federal Judge Charles Moye, requested from Glass's attorney a list of character witnesses so the jurors could be asked if they knew any of these names. Glass's attorney stated that he had spoken with Senator Herman Talmadge, Speaker of the House Tom Murphy's. Culver Kidd and Georgia Chief Justice. Kelley Quillian of the Georgia Court of Appeal, who all had agreed to testify.

Sheriff Glass appealed his conviction but lost his appeal. Mr. Glass passed away on April 25, 2013.

8
Deadly Drug Deal

Marietta, GA 3-6-1984 Defendants:

1. Patrick Daniel Connor
Conspiracy to Purchase Cocaine- Attempted Robbery, (deceased)

2. William "Angel" Pabon
Conspiracy to Purchase & Distribute Cocaine - Guilty

3. Daniel Wayne Garrett
Conspiracy to Purchase Cocaine - Guilty

4. Sheila Patricia Robinson
Guilty - Conspiracy to Purchase Cocaine.

One of the most feared incidents in Narcotic Investigations is a drug undercover investigation gone bad. This case shows how dangerous Undercover work is!

While I was sitting at my desk, Agent Chuck Crane entered my office and advised me that he had a CI (Confidential Informant) who arranged a meeting with a group of drug traffickers living in Cobb County. These individuals approached the CI, inquiring if he could introduce them to someone who could sell. three kilograms of cocaine.

Chuck stated that the meet was set up by us to do a reverse sting on these guys and arrest them when they delivered the cocaine after we did a quick surprised show of $156,000 for the purchase of three kilos of cocaine. We contacted Sgt. Jimmy Maxwell, head of the Cobb County Sheriff's Department and who is on board with his agent to assist and arrest them.

Chuck said, "I will be the undercover agent meeting these guys and S/A Don Augustine (aka "Diego") will show up unannounced and show the cocaine, to the suspect and drive off once it is shown! The surveillance team will consist of Agent Bob Michelotti, Ray Stasney (deceased), Ron Metcalf (deceased), Larry Sproat, you! And Maxwell's team will be Sgt. Maxwell, Deputy Hass, and Sgt. Wayne Kelly. The team was briefed and are already there to set their surveillance spot. The meeting place is at Charlie's Place Bar, parking lot which faces US –41 Cobb Parkway. You will be with Sgt Maxwell, Sgt Wayne Kelley and Ron Metcalf across the street parked facing the bar parking lot, parked under a covered roof. The owner gave Sgt. Maxwell permission to park there. We got one hour before the meeting!"

"Chuck, you got this extremely well organized. Wait here, I'll brief Buzz and we're off!"

The team was told that no one was to move in unless Chuck was in danger and all units notified and given a go.

As pre-arranged, we all took our spots to discreetly observe the meeting. Chuck was already parked in the third parking slot from the one way in the lot. He was standing outside his vehicle which was backed up in the space, drinking a bottled beer. The suspect arrived and lowered the passenger window then Chuck leaned down and was speaking with the suspect.

As planned, Diego drove in, stopped, and held up a bag, showing the suspect the money, and drove off as planned.

The suspect in the car drove off and went west on Cobb Parkway, followed by me as we observed him pulling into a Walmart parking lot, and stopped next to a Cadillac driven by a female, later identified as Sheila Robinson. She proceeded to get out of the car and open the trunk as the male driver and a male passenger, got out of their car and walked to the back of the Cadillac, where the female handed them pistols. The female got back in her car and stayed while the two males left to go back to the bar.

I immediately advised all the team that the suspects just got guns from a female. "All units, suspects picked up guns. This could be a rip off, be prepared and alert!"

The driver returned and backed in beside Crane's vehicle. Crane still holding a beer bottle was standing against the front right headlight and walked behind the right side of his car while the two suspects had gotten out of the car, both standing and greeting Chuck between the two cars. Chuck's back was toward the high weed field.

Sgt. Kelley from our surveillance spot was watching this with binoculars and observed Chuck with his hands up and holding his beer bottle, and slowly backing up toward the field. Chuck later advised that the passenger Garrett had a gun pointed at him and was forcing him to walk into the woods prior to Connor striking him.

Suddenly over the radio, one of the surveillance agents yelled, "Move in now! They got a gun on Chuck!"

I immediately yelled on the radio, "No, hold still! Chucks got it under control!" At which time observed by Kelly, was Connor dressed in a blue denim jacket, who came out of the brush behind Chuck, striking him with what appeared to be a metal object!

(Chuck later said, "I saw out of the corner of my eyes that Connor was about to strike me, and I immediately slightly moved my head to the left and sustained a glancing blow then immediately smacked Garrett with my beer bottle on the left side of the face and leaped over the trunk of the car with my bottle to run for cover.")

I immediately yelled over the radio for all units, "Move in now!" Having the car running, I immediately floored the gas pedal and had a clear, traffic path and took it, stopping short to the left front of the Monte Carlo which was being cranked up to start. We all jumped out of the car. I immediately went toward the driver Garret, pointing my Walther PPKS 9mm. Garrett looked at me and started to raise his right hand with a gun slightly turning towards me to shoot me through the glass window. I knew that I had to shoot, my aim being right at his head. I fired 7 shots directly at his head from approximately three feet, but the bullets never penetrated the new Plexiglass window. Garrett immediately screeched out of his parking spot, turned right, went around the building and stopped, facing Sgt. Jimmy Maxwell and DEA agents with pointed pistols at his head, causing him to surrender immediately.

The passenger Connor had run back into the woods chased by Deputy Hass and Sgt. Kelley. Garrett was apprehended by the DEA team. I immediately proceeded to search for Connor when suddenly I heard a shotgun and yelled, "Are you okay?"

Kelly responded, "Yes! Over here!"

As I approached, I heard a second shot. Kelley advised me, that he observed Connor pointing a gun at Deputy Hass who was standing and fired a shot that struck Connor and caused him to flip down in the weeds. Kelley ran to him advising him that he would get help for him and to get his hands up. As he approached Connor, he saw him raising his right hand holding onto a pistol. It was at this moment when he shot him again, and the suspect died on the scene.

The crime scene was secured and thank God all our team were safe. Chuck sustained a large bruise, and the assault weapon was a large steel wrench found at the scene. Within 15 minutes, our friend Sheriff Bill Hudson arrived with his detective chief. He approached me and spoke, "Pete, is everyone okay?"

I replied, "Yes! Thank God! It was a rip off… for the money and clean shot, Bill! I fired seven shots with my PPK at the driver who attempted to shoot me, and not one damn bullet penetrated the Plexiglass window! Thank God!"

Everyone went home safely, which goes to show that our job is not an average job in law enforcement. It's highly dangerous, and we are aware of the high risk associated with this unique job.

* * *

Returning to the office, the SAIC Ray Vinsick and ASAIC Buzz Derrell were fully briefed. I returned to my office where the group was waiting for me for a full debriefing.

Chuck addressed the group saying, "This was a close call, guys! I kept my composure and saw my break and took swift action. You guys moved in swiftly, and I thought for sure this was it for me. You're the best, my friends! I'm proud to be part of this amazing team. I know you were probably saying to yourself when I told you all not to move in, 'What the fuck is he doing? Chuck needs help now!' Yes! He did but having been held hostage with a gun by a NY Puerto Rican delivering a kilo of coke to me in Ft. Lauderdale and accusing me to be a cop, one of the agents surveilling me said the same thing on the radio to move in! Some of you may know Nick Navarro, ex- FBN Agent/ FDLE (Florida Department of Law Enforcement Agent, and Sheriff of Broward Count, FL.(deceased) was furnishing the buy money and immediately yelled, 'No, Pete, will talk his way out. Stand down!' Nick saved my life that day had they moved in. This Wacko had been arrested several times for attempted murder/ aggravated assault with intent to kill in NY. I convinced him that I was not a cop and he started making phone calls to my CI, whose father was a Mobster in Ft. Lauderdale, who could verify my story, and the deal was successfully made. The suspect was arrested that night at his ex-wife's house. I later learned after leaving for France, that this SOB had killed his wife while still awaiting trial.

"When interviewed he admitted that if he had proven that I was a cop, he would have killed me immediately. I felt that Chuck was experienced in undercover work and trained over the years on how to swiftly analyze the danger and take swift action! It's amazing how your adrenaline kicks into high gear.

"All I can say is that it's experience and knowing that your team is behind you!

Okay! Go home and write your reports on your actions on this case surveillance for the next two days and be on call and enjoy your family or others. You deserve this. "JOB WELL DONE ALL!"

We all laughed and relaxed together for a while and went our way home.

There were many cases made during my being assigned with this fantastic group of agents. Due to the influx of cases being made, a new enforcement group was formed with eight agents and a new group supervisor named Ernie Howard.

9
Southern Comfort

**Conspiracy to import cocaine into the United States
June 1982 to September 1983**

4 Major seizures of cocaine totaling 2,668.4 pounds

**14 Documented shipments of cocaine totaling
8,000 pounds of pure cocaine.**

Brief Summary of case:

This case started June 1992 because of information received from a confidential source (CI) alerting us that a DEA fugitive named Harold Rosenthal, arranged to have a shipment of Cocaine flown in from Colombia, delivered to a hired driver in Rockwood, Tennessee, at a motel for transportation to Florida. The shipment was 1250 pounds of cocaine, which was the largest single seizure documented in the U.S. at that time. It ended with the seizure and arrest of five defendants armed with Uzi machine guns. Our group began this investigation, and for the next 16 months this case involved dangerous undercover work and surveillance in Georgia, Tennessee, (Chattanooga, Rockwood), Crystal River, Florida, Ft. Lauderdale, Pembroke Pines, FL. Atlanta, Reading, The Bahamas and South Florida, California, Arkansas, and Oklahoma.

The leaders of this drug smuggling were fugitive Harold Rosenthal cocaine smuggler, being protected in Medellin, Colombia, by Pablo Escobar. Rosenthal was the broker for the

U.S. Mobster Charlie Alamo (aka "Wing") and Phillip Bonadonna of Coral Spring, Florida who were members of the NY Gambino Mob!

This entire investigation became so massive and dangerous during which situations occurred when orders were given to kill our undercover pilot and the Colombian Attorney General Lora Bonilla. This case will be covered in detail in part two of this book.

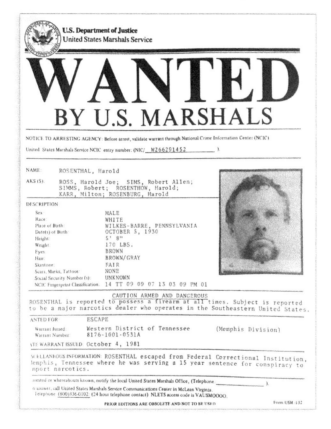

U.S. Department of Justice Wanted Poster Harold Rosenthal

Rosenthal attempted to escape custody again and sadly for him, I was one step ahead of him and foiled his attempt by being undercover with him.

The announcement of the arrest of all 30 defendants was

done in person in Atlanta by the Attorney General of the United States William French Smith, stating "The Federal Grand Jury indicted 30 members of a drug trafficking ring that smuggled some five tons of cocaine into the United States with a street value of $3.8 billion dollars. Measured by the number of drugs, it is the largest cocaine trafficking ring ever broken up in the history of Federal Law Enforcement, the Attorney General said in his Press Conference in Atlanta.

This investigation was the first DEA case to be merged to the newly formed Organized Crime Drug Enforcement Task Force created by President Reagan. I was advised that I had been selected by DEA to be the DEA's Criminal OCDE Task Force Coordinator effective 8-9-83.

Attorney General and new OCDE Task Force Coordinators

We became the transporter for the U.S. mob and received one million dollars to purchase a 'stash house' in Paulding County as well as vehicles to transport the cocaine to Ft. Lauderdale. Subsequently, I was moved to the Atlanta Federal Court Building and continued these massive investigations and appointed as the DEA Criminal Investigator / Representative to the newly created Presidential Organized Crime Task Force ordered by President Reagan. During this assignment, I was appointed and remained responsible for the total domestic and international coordination of case G-3-83-Zool Operation Southern Comfort and the supervision of the Title III operation of this case and arrest of Harold Rosenthal in South America. This case was proclaimed The Largest Cocaine Conspiracy in the United States History. This was also the first joint DEA/FBI/US Customs/Alcohol and Tobacco/U.S. Marshal, State and Local Law Enforcement Agents, Title III case ever initiated, which involved the participation of over 50 federal agents, and approximately 25 State and local agents throughout the U.S.

10
OCDE Task Force Coordinator
9-12-1983 to 1-30-1985

My last day as DEA Supervisor was emotional for me because our team was not only the best, but we were a family. A few months prior to being replaced, my great secretary Patty had a baby boy and left to be a mother at home. Her position was advertised in the DEA Vacancy Program. Our file clerk Andy asked to meet with me and shut the door.

"What's up, Andy? Have a seat."

"Pete, I've known you for several years and consider you   a great boss for all of us. As you know, I was a College English Professor at Emery University, and due to budget cuts and being the low man in seniority, I was honorably dismissed because of cuts in the budget."

"Yeah, Andy, I'm sure that was a real shocker for you!"

"Pete, I'll get to the point why I'm here; I saw that Patty had to leave and her position has been advertised. I want that job and would be honored to work for you as your secretary!" he blurted out smiling.

I looked at him and saw that he was honest about this and really wanted this position.

"Andy, how are your typing skills? You know that with close to 18 people doing reports and all, it's a demanding job?"

"Pete, I can type faster than any other secretary in this office and because of my English degree, it's without any errors the first time on documents," he smiled.

"Andy, I believe you, my friend, and I am honored that you asked for this, and the decision is mine only! I will advise Ray to call D.C. and withdraw the vacancy announcement. I am honored to have you; the job is yours!" I added as we shook hands.

"Pete, thank you so much. I will be faithful and if I am not wrong, we made DEA history just now, on my being the first male secretary in DEA!" He smiled with big grin of joy. Always being the fun guy, he continued, "Pete, I expect you to treat me just like any other secretary. By the way, Secretary Week is coming up, and I expect flowers and lunch with all of you, just like you did for Patty."

"Andy, you got yourself a deal," I responded while laughing out loud!

Later that day I met with Buzz and Ray to tell them that one of our employees asked me for the secretary's position, and I accepted. "I would like for you to call HQ Personnel Director and cancel the vacancy announcement!"

Ray asked, "Who did you get?"

"Ray, I hired Andy our filing clerk!"

Ray with a stunned look said, "You know you're the first in DEA to get a male secretary. Be prepared to be harassed about this!"

With a wink of the eye I said, "Yes, I know. What can I say?" I Laughed out loud as I walked back to my office.

Andy was standing in front of the file room when I said, "Come with me now! Walking into the group I began, "Listen up, everyone, I have an announcement for you!" Turning to Andy, I continued, "Meet your new group secretary, our friend Andy!" Everyone started clapping with joy and came over to shake his hand and welcome him to our gang! What a great moment! After leaving Atlanta 1 1/2 years later, Andy became Ray's secretary.

The new group supervisor was one of my best friends "Jimmy Guy" whom I worked with on the French Connection case and was the Country Attaché in Belgium. (R.I.P. my good friend).

There were twelve of us OCDETF Coordinators in the U.S. and we were responsible to insure and coordinate DEA's participation in the OCDE program. The Task force Agency Coordinators were ATF Fred Woodward; FBI-Richard Dean; IRS Del Butler; U.S. Attorneys Craig Gillen, Gordon Miller, Steve Wisebram, Buddy Baker, and Larry Thompson; U.S. Marshal Bob Darnell; U.S. Customs, Bob Holloway.

I was also responsible to coordinate the activities of agents assigned to the Task Force on cases that were accepted by us.

We worked with the U.S. Attorney Larry Thompson and his Assistant Attorney's Task Force Coordinator and 11 Coordinators throughout the U.S.

I also worked with DEA on Southern Comfort in undercover actions, etc. I remained fully involved with this case and travelled on several occasions to conduct surveillance on Harold Rosenthal in Barranquilla. Colombia and Medellin to plan for his removal with Country Attachés Miguel Vahill of Medellin and Herb Williams of Barranquilla (Story will be in part two: Southern Comfort.)

I briefed the SAIC Ray Vinsick on all activities of cases and assisted the ASAIC and RAIC in determining the need, for search warrants and the stage at which to conduct searches, make seizures, and apprehend and arrest suspected violators. I also worked with SAIC/ ASAIC to insure in the district the full effective participation of DEA investigators in multi-agency cases.

The position assignment was determined by ensuring that the person selected for this position had in-depth knowledge and expertise in law enforcement at a Local, State and Federal Level, and serve as DEA's representative onsite and exercise reasoned judgement in all contacts with the media and community.

Numerous investigations were made and after a year and half, to my surprise, I received on January 30, 1985, a transfer assignment from Washington HQ to be assigned to Cocaine Desk as a Staff Coordinator, in Washington D.C.

This assignment was required for all Grade 14 Supervisors to do Management Training in HQ for a minimum of two years. The assignment title was called 'Desk Officer' for various Drug Departments. Real Agents had a name for this assignment as 'The Kiss of Death.'

Timing was bad since, I had just bought a house and we loved living in Georgia. One must do and serve at the pleasure of God and Country and smile! Washington, here I come!!

11
DEA Washington Headquarters
Staff Coordinator, Cocaine Division
1-25-1984 to 7-03-1984

Reporting to DEA HQ was quite an experience for 4 years. My wife and kids had to remain behind and sell our home in Cobb County which took several months. To my amazement, SAIC Ray Vinsick also received orders to be transferred as the Chief of the Marijuana Desk. We both shared an apartment in Maryland until we purchased our homes.

I reported to the Cocaine Chief John Phelps at the DEA HQ which was located at 14th and I street, NW, 3 blocks from the White House. There I was introduced to staff coordinators, Lou Perry and John Constanza and was told that I would share an office with John Constanza. John and I had a great time working together and tried to get used to this new environment.

The job description for a staff coordinator consisted of reviewing division's work plans as it pertains to cocaine enforcement worldwide, evaluating and obtaining approval for funding expenditures, flash rolls, reverse undercover operations, and Title III operations (Wire Taps) as well as special enforcement operations matters requiring headquarters' concurrence at the highest levels of management.

On December 4, 1984, I was assigned to be the Staff Coordinator for Operation BUSCON (SEO 520) which was initiated for the purpose of locating and arresting the most important Colombian extraditable fugitives, i.e., Pablo Escobar and Carlos Ledher.

During this operation I was responsible for alerting and assisting various field elements during the months of January and February, when DEA was being threatened by Colombian traffickers and participated in HQ briefings to the Administrator and Deputy Administrator during this phase of the operation.

One of our responsibilities was to answer Congressional Inquiries from members of Congress and do briefings to Congressman Charles Rangel who was head of the Narcotic Committee. The briefing was done by DEA, U.S. Customs, Coast Guard, and the State Department. After attending several of these briefings, Congressman Rangel started the briefing session in rotation from left to right at the table. I always sat as last person to speak. When it got to be my turn, Rangel said, "Mr. Charette, how are you doing? I bet you miss France, right?

"Yes, I do sir, and I enjoyed taking you and your wife around Paris!"

"Pete, those were good days! Okay, Pete, you heard these fine gentlemen give their assessment. How about you now? Tell me the real story. You never hesitate to tell it like it is!"

"Congressman, I appreciate the opportunity to tell it like it is!" For 20 minutes I briefed him on the real story as to where we stood with our efforts, but it differed from what was presented. I never patronized anyone, and I firmly believed that if you told the truth, you would never be challenged.

The looks of daggers in their eyes were obvious, fully knowing that they resented my presence at these briefings. After the meeting concluded, Mr. Rangel came over, shook my hand and thanked me for being upfront with my presentation.

I returned to my office where the Deputy Chief Tony said, "Pete, Rangel transmitted us that you did a great job! We received a few calls by these disgruntled agencies that you need to be in sync with them!"

"Tony, all I can say is "Ba Fungo to them!" I laughed.

The most tragic moment of my career happened while working at the Cocaine Desk when on February 7, 1985, we received an alert that one of our agents had been kidnapped in Mexico by the Mexican Cartel Chief Angel Felix Gallardo. We were told that the agent was Enrique "Kiki" Camarena, a friend of all of us and best agent assigned to Mexico.

The Director assigned a Task Force to work in our conference room where we learned that Kiki died on February 9, after 30 hours of brutal torturing by Gallardo's people. I will never forget that during the start of this investigation. The SOB's sent a recorded tape of his torture to DEA. Director Jack Lawn and the group listened to this horrific torturing and all expressed disbelief of this horrible act.

Working in this division was great, but I had asked the head of Foreign Operation Ray McKinnon (deceased) to put me in his division, since he had an opening and had indicated that he wanted me. He requested my reassignment to his division which was immediately granted for me to report on July 3, 1984.

12
Staff Coordinator
International Programs Staff
4-23-84 To 7-3-84

My assignment to this division was exactly the area of expertise to which I wanted to contribute. My duties consisted of monitoring, coordinating and evaluating DEA drug suppression programs and special projects in Country and Resident Offices as assigned.

One of my duties was to serve as interpreter for the director when French dignitaries came to visit and meet with our director and department heads.

I enjoyed my three-month assignment and selected new Country Attachés for foreign assignments and visited Canada to meet with the head of the Canadian Mounties in Montreal, to discuss cooperation on investigations.

The reason for the short assignment occurred when I had lunch with my great friend Phil Perry (RIP) and Mark Markman (RIP) from Internal Affairs Division. During our luncheon, Mark who was the Chief of Internal Affairs said, "Pete, I have a vacancy announcement coming out for an IA Investigator Grade 15. Phil and I have been discussing who to select to be part of our team, and we all agreed that you were the one that is fit for this position. We would love to have you, and would you be willing to apply for this vacancy?"

"Mark, Phil you guys caught me off guard. I am honored for

you confidence in me, and I accept your offer."

"Pete," Mark responded, "The vacancy comes out tomorrow so apply for it. You have earned this because your integrity is beyond reproach, and you have our respect." We then all finished lunch.

The selection announcement was made two days later, and I was promoted to Grade 15 on July 3, 1984.

This promotion brought me to the height of my career. It took me a while to fully accept that I had moved to this plateau. I was honored and proud that not once did I kiss ass to get to this level. I worked hard and paid the price at times, near death.

13
Promotion Criminal Investigator
Planning and Inspection Division, Washington D.C.
7-3-84 To 5-02-88

I reported to work across the street from HQ to work at the office of Chief Mark Markman. As I entered the office, I was greeted by Mark and the team which consisted of Agents Phil Perry, Bill Slowick, Frank Panessa, Vern Parker and Tom O'Grady. We all went to Mark's office who briefed us. "Pete, you are now one of us, and I'm proud to have you on our team! We are all friends and work together as a team, and all our cases remain discreet, not to be disclosed to anyone unless directed by me to do so. The way I expect all the inspectors to approach an allegation of any agents is by always approaching it on the premise that the individual is not guilty until proven guilty. This may be strange to you because we have always heard or seen Internal Affairs Investigators immediately assume that the alleged person is guilty first. That approach is absurd and won't be tolerated in this unit by me. With that said, you will share an office with crazy Tom!" Tom was a great agent who loved to joke around with the team, and I learned a lot with all the team members, who jumped in immediately giving me tips on doing this type of investigation.

I had been exposed to work with Internal Affair Inspectors Phil Perry and Vern Parker, who had requested that I assist them in an investigation in Mississippi and New Orleans that involved a possible murder of a female stripper in New Orleans by owners of a strip club on Bourbon Street. A DEA agent was alleged to have full knowledge of this and withheld reporting that the body was dumped off a bridge in Mississippi.

A DEA agent was implicated by a source of information to IA (Internal Affair). Phil asked for me since he was aware that I had experience in homicide investigation when I worked as a detective. I was briefed on this, and the investigation led us to an identified suspect involved in this crime who was incarcerated in Parchment Prison (Louisiana Penitentiary). We were able to interview this person who, after several hours of questioning, admitted to having participated in this murder and that the DEA agent was knowledgeable of this and was implicated by this suspect. This led to his removal as an agent, and the information was given to the New Orleans/Mississippi Police.

IA Investigators have tremendous authority given to them, to use their skills, to investigate agents, and agency management and in-line personnel. A must for selection is that you must have had prior experience as a law enforcement officer for this position.

One great satisfaction in this type of work is being able to prove that an agent is falsely accused and you're able to show that the accuser did this to hurt the agent's reputation.

I was called to Mark's office and asked to sit in on a briefing by a State Department and a U.S. Department of Justice Attorney and to listen to the entire briefing. Mark stated that he wanted me there because of my overseas experience, and once the briefing was completed, he wanted my opinion on this allegation.

Mark instructed his secretary to bring the guest in, and he introduced me as one of his international inspectors.

The briefing was about one of our country offices in the Far East where they had identified one of our agents as a suspect who vouched for foreign national officials to obtain visas to the U.S. for relatives of the head of this country's State Department Director. (For the protection of this agent, the names, office and country will be withheld). Their investigation disclosed that the foreign politician was charging the alleged relatives hundreds of dollars for the Visas.

State Department Investigator stated that they had interviewed some of the alleged relatives and some could not be found. The DOJ attorney chimed in advising that they were ready to indict this agent and furnished a copy of their report to Mark.

Once the presentation ended, Mark asked me what my opinions were on the facts presented.

"Mark, I thank these official for their work on this matter, but I am baffled that some of the alleged family members could not be located. I request that I be permitted with Frank Panessa and this gentleman from State Department to go with us to locate the persons who had not been interviewed. Also, it's my understanding that this foreign official was also this agent's Godmother for his baby! This person has not been interviewed! Why? Allegations of this sort are serious, and this investigation needs more work. I hope you're not offended by my frankness, but I call it as I see it, and given the country's reputation for corruption, this smells to me and needs to be thoroughly investigated. I ask that we go together and hold off for two weeks before proceeding with charges."

Mark responded, "Pete, thank you, and I concur with Pete's assessment and ask that we pursue it further. We are talking about someone's career, and he deserves to be fully exonerated if that's the case! Pete, thank you. You can leave now; I'll be with you shortly."

"Yes, sir! Pleasure meeting you and hope we will travel together as soon as possible!"

I was asked to meet with Mark who said, "Make your flight arrangements for two weeks in the Far East and a State Department representative will have someone at the embassy assigned to help you. Make sure you call the Country Attaché and let him know your flight and arrival time, and to get a hotel near the office and embassy. Pete, good job!"

"If the AUSA had not gone with the plan, then I would have made one phone call to DOJ

Assistant Deputy General Boykin Rose who would have slammed the breaks and put this on hold for us!"

"Jesus, is there anyone, that you don't know?"

"Yep! The pope!" We all laughed.

* * *

Frank Panessa and I flew to the Far East and arrived at the airport. Waiting for us was the DEA Country Attaché. We checked into our hotel and immediately went to his office. We briefed him about the allegations by State Department and he advised that he was made aware of this, and his agent has not been notified.

We then proceeded to the embassy and met with the passport chief and briefed him about the alleged allegations we were furnished against the persons who received these visas from the Country's State Department Director.

* * *

For the next three days, we tracked down these individuals; some were related to her, and some were not, and they admitted paying her to get visas for them to visit relatives in the U.S. Once we received this confirmation and admission that they had no direct contact with our agents, it became apparent that she used her friendship to mislead our agent, that these were her relatives, and he assumed that she was being honest. This practice was common around the world as a diplomatic service to the host country leaders.

Once we had our data and findings, we asked the country attaché, to have the agent meet us in the conference room alone without his presence. The agent greeted us, and we introduced ourselves to him. Frank started interviewing him and advised him of the allegation against him.

He immediately spoke up saying that he could not believe

that this female country director could have done this, using their long-trusted friendship. He stated that he had done this with numerous law enforcement officers who asked for visas to travel to the U.S. on vacation with families.

He was extremely hurt that he had been misled by this woman and asked that they get her to come to this office to confront her openly about having used him to make money for herself by selling visa access from him. We could tell that he was being honest with us, and we agreed to let us confront her.

The country attaché was asked to call, this woman and ask her to come to his office regarding an important matter that couldn't be done over the phone. Within thirty minutes she arrived, and he introduced us and told her we needed to discuss some important matters with her. She agreed and proceeded to the conference room.

Frank advised that this interview was being recorded and conducted the interview. Once he told her of this allegation against our agent, she stiffened up and her body language immediately showed that she was, in my opinion, in over her head.

Frank told her she was a suspect in selling visas to her family and friends and misrepresenting and falsifying why she was asking our agent for favors, fully knowing she was lying to him.

She was advised that this matter could be resolved in two ways: First, that she agreed to resign immediately from her government position, and this matter would be close immediately. Second, that if she refused, then this would be immediately reported to the head of her government, the prime minister and the media.

She immediately chose to resign and sincerely apologized for what she did to this agent and immediately left crying.

Frank and I looked at each other and smiled with joy that we had saved this great agent from being charged. To this day, he has remained a friend and had a great career.

There were many more cases, but the one that I will never

be forget was a case that involved a special agent in charge of a major field office in the U.S. This occurred after Mark was made the Director of Supervising the new construction of the DEA HQ in Crystal City. Appointed in his place was Peter Gruden, a great respected friend by all.

I had been briefed by the director that I was selected by him to do a sensitive investigation against a special agent in charge, of a major division in the field who was abusing his power by violating improper travel regulations, misuses of rental vehicles and wrongful travel vouchers. The director asked that this not be discussed with anyone. I accepted his assignment, and Tom O'Grady and I left town to conduct this investigation.

Someone in this office had informed the director and our boss that this person was misusing his authority and needed to be investigated. Tom and I both knew that this was not going to be pleasant since this person was well known in DEA. We both had a job to do, and rank had no bearing on us.

We met with the person who had uncovered this misuse of office. During the interview, this person presented copies of records that pertained to these allegations. A review of the documents directly revealed proof that the allegations were legitimate. We notified the boss Peter that the documents clearly proved misuses of government funds and abuse of authority. Peter informed us to proceed and to interview him now.

We requested that his secretary tell the SAIC we would like to meet with him in the conference room and to hold his calls. The SAIC came in the room with his secretary and stated to our surprise that he had been expecting us and had gotten word that he was under investigation. He further advised that his secretary will be present and take notes of this interview. He was arrogant and never had the courtesy to shake our hands.

I informed him why we were here, and that we had conducted interviews with some of his staff and agents to which he replied that he was aware. I informed him that the Administrator of DEA assigned us to investigate the allegations and therefore, we hoped that he would assist us in clarifying these matters.

The individual informed us that he did not have to speak with us and started to leave. Tommy immediately said to him, "Hold up and sit down! Now!"

He responded, "Who in the hell are you to tell me to sit down?" Tommy said, "You either sit down or you are ordered to be in

Washington Internal Affairs Office tomorrow at 10:00 a.m." "You can't order me!"

Tommy and I both got up and said, "See you tomorrow in D.C.! Mr. Gruden will be waiting for you!"

We both left, caught a flight back home, and advised Pete Gruden who said, "Great job, both of you, I will be waiting for him. See you in the morning."

The next morning this SAIC walked into our office front door and escorted into Mr. Gruden's office. Pete asked us to go back to our office and asked this SAIC to have a seat.

There was some loud discussion going on which at times could be heard. After that meeting, I was told that the administrator wanted to see me. I went and met with the administrator and briefed him. He was surprised when I told him that someone had alerted him that he was being investigated by IA. I told the administrator that I would find out where the leak was.

I made some phone calls and got my answer and advised Peter who then advised the administrator.

The result of this investigation was that this SAIC had to repay money that was misused and retired later. This was a perfect example that the system worked, and that everyone was treated the same as others.

Returning from the trip, I reported back to Peter on a Monday morning, "Hey Peter! Feels good to be back!"

"Don't sit down. The boss across the street wants to see you now!"

"What's up?"

"You will find out soon enough!"

"Oh shit, I'll be back," I responded shaking my head. Then I left and proceeded to the administrator's office.

The administrator said, "Come on in, Pete, sit down. We need to talk about something!"

"I swear, boss, I've been a good boy" I mused with a nervous laugh.

"Pete, I hate to break this to you, but I am transferring you and five other grade 15s to be ASAIC'S in the Miami Field Division. Tom Cash is putting his team together and called me and said he wanted you specifically and the rest was our call. I know that Janice will not be happy. Cash said he needs you. Liaison needs to be fixed and local chiefs and sheriffs have asked for you!"

"Jack, you're going to tell her, not me!" I laughed. "She was your secretary when you were an FBI agent!"

"You tell Tom Cash that once again he wants me to make him look good!"

"Okay, boss, I'm in!"

Now, I knew why Peter was in a bad mood. I walked back in and went to his office where we both had laughs even though I was sad to go, but it was time for me to go back where "The Ride" all began.

14
Miami Field Division
Assistant Special Agent in Charge
5/12/1988 to 12/19/1993

My first day coming to work at the Kroger Complex next to the Doral Golf Course in Miami felt great, back to where the "Ride" being an agent first began.

I reported to the SAIC Tom Cash, who was awaiting my arrival. Tom welcomed me. "Well, Mr. Charette, you finally made it! Welcome to Miami," and he shook my hand.

"Tom, I am here to make you great, and Janice wants to kill you!" Both of us laughed. Tom and his wife Peggy were great friends of ours, and we couldn't wait to get together again.

"Pete, your friends are in the conference room waiting for us for the Monday morning team meeting!"

As we entered, the team said, "He's here!" Then they all greeted me. Present were ASAIC's Asst. SAIC Lionel Stewart, Asst. SAIC John Phelps, ASAICs Low Perry, Bill Henson, Al Coward, Anthony Bocchicchio, Charles Lutz and Jerry Hockman (aka "The Hawk"). Every one of them, I had worked with in Washington D.C. headquarters and were great friends. There was no doubt in my mind that we were going to kick bad guys' asses. Everyone in that room to me were the best of the best from the old days when agents were ass kicking agents.

Cash started the meeting by advising us that the team was finally together and that the assignment of each one of us was as follows:

- Johnny Phelps- In Charge of ASAIC Coward, Anthony Bocchicchio, and Administration
- Lionel Stewart (deceased) Deputy Assistant in Charge- In Charge of Perry (Ft. Lauderdale RO and West Palm Beach Resident Office).
- Henson (In charge of Miami Group Supervisors)
- Charles Lutz (in charge of Caribbean Offices).
- Pierre Charette- In Charge of Resident Offices in State of Florida (Marathon, Orlando, Gainesville, Tallahassee, Jacksonville, Panama City Tampa, Fort Myers.

Tom assured us that he will support us any way possible to ensure that we make this division number one in the nation. He stated that he was proud of this team and was confident we would make it work. He also insisted that liaison with state and local law enforcement was the number one priority.

I was shown the location of my office on the second floor of this building. We had four buildings in this business development.

My secretary Anita filled me in and was the best. In a meeting with Lionel, he instructed me that there were some major liaison issues with my division that needed my attention. He assured me that he fully supported me, and that Tom had briefed him that I would handle it properly.

I advised him that this was my number one priority and would leave shortly to visit all offices in the state and meet with the local law enforcement chiefs and sheriffs.

For a month I met with all resident agents of my offices and had great success in outlining what our expectations were, and that liaison was the number one priority with case making. I insured all my RAIC's that they call the shots on investigations, and I was there to support them 100% and not to ever lie to me because that would be the "Kiss of Death." The message was strong and fully understood.

I also reviewed all the case logs and informant logs and pointed my concerns about agents who appeared to be riding the shirttails of the case makers. I instructed them to have a "Come to Jesus" meeting with these agents and give them orders that they were expected to initiate cases on their own and whose performances I would review in 90 days. If no improvement was seen, then we would find them a home somewhere else in another field office in the U.S. This was not to be a threat, but a promise. If they had a good liaison with their local counterparts, then cases would be made. It was RAIC's and my responsibility to ensure compliance.

The word spread like wildfire, and some RAIC's did not appreciate my presence, which was confided to me by various agents in confidence. As Tom used to say to me, "Mr. Charette, just remember that 'No good deed goes unpunished.'"

All offices listed were outstanding in case making, and during my overseeing this division, our team offices seized several thousands of kilograms of cocaine.

Our Jacksonville Resident Office worked the case against the famous Colombian Drug Lord Carlos Lehder, co-founder of the Medellin Cartel, who was the first kingpin in Colombia deported to the U.S. for prosecution. The trial was held in Federal Court in Jacksonville and our RAIC Jerry Rhinehart (deceased), who was a close friend, attended the trial. Lehder was found guilty of smuggling thousands of pounds of cocaine through the Bahamas destined to the Florida coast. He served 33 years and 4 months but was originally sentenced to life imprisonment plus 135 years commuted to 55 years for drug trafficking in prison and was released from federal prison, on June 16, 2020. In 1992, Lehder agreed to testify against Manuel Noriega. As a result, his sentence was reduced to 55 years. The Jacksonville office was one of the best in Florida. (RIP Jerry)

In this position every day brought new cases and problems that demanded immediate actions.

15
Fire Bombing of a DEA Office
FT. Myers, Florida
March 18, 1990

The phone rang while we were at home fast asleep. My wife answered it. "Hi, Brian. Hold on."

"Pete, Brian Rafferty on the phone."

"Brian, what's up at 2 a.m.?"

"Pete, someone bombed our office to the ground!"

"What? Are you putting me on!"

"Frog, it's no joke. We need you to fly in ASAP. The FBI and local police got this place roped off!

Okay, pal, I'll get the Air Wing to fly me in. I'll be there in an hour and a half!"

"Oh! The FBI is here. Someone called them, and they said they are taking over now."

"Brian, Listen to me. They have jurisdiction since it's considered federal property. Tell whoever is in charge that I am coming down now, and no one is to discuss this with the media, and that we will schedule a press conference for 10 a.m. at the steps of the courthouse and keep onlookers 100 yards from the scene."

"Gotcha, Frog. See you soon."

"Okay! We will land on the field to the left of your office. Clear everyone from there for us to land!" I ordered.

Bombed building/ RAIC /ASAIC

"Okay!"

I immediately called Joe Bock, head of our Air Wing Office at Opa-Locka Airport. I advised him that I would be picking him up, and we would fly with one of our helicopters ASAP. Joe lived two blocks from me and was waiting outside of his home. We headed to the Municipal Airport with siren blasting and blue light flashing. We made it in 25 minutes and one of Joe's chopper pilots had already cranked up the helicopter and off we lifted to cross the Everglades for Fort Myers' DEA office on the West Coast of Florida.

Approaching the office from the air, we could see a bunch of police blue lights, firetrucks red lights, and numerous unmarked cars at the scene. We also detected a large funnel of black smoke rising in the sky!

"Holy Shit!" we said at the same time as we started to land.

I called Lionel and Tom Cash and appraised them of the situation. I told Tom that the FBI was on the scene, and they had told Brian that they now oversaw this investigation!

Tom said, "Frenchy, diplomacy, my friend!"

"Tom, I am a diplomat trained by you. Have no fear. I got a plan already worked out in my head. Everything will be done by our book. Get my drift?"

"Got it. Keep me posted!"

"Roger that! Frog out!"

We landed and Brian made the introductions. The FBI chief then advised me that they were taking over the crime scene for which I thanked him.

"I will make sure that we assign an agent with each member of your team to ensure that what's left of our property is tagged and photographed, along with what's left of our files. I'm sure you understand that if the shoe was on your foot, you would do the same as to what we're asking!" He immediately agreed to this request.

Brian and I got together, and he briefed me that earlier before closing the office, one of his agents observed as he walked out the front door to a roundabout street, a vehicle driving at a slow speed and both passengers staring at our agent. The agent recognized them as being two brothers who had been previously arrested. The driver was a Jeffrey Matthews, 23 years of age, and his brother John Ciganek, 22 years of age. Brian stated that his agent came back into the office and advised him that Matthews was checking them out. Information had been received by several sources that after being indicted, Matthews had passed the word around that he was going to damage the DEA office. Matthews called the DEA office threatening to damage it.

On March 15, 1990, he was indicted with three other defendants charged with distributing cocaine. Two days later, the office in the morning hours at 2:00 a.m. was blown up with a pipe bomb packed with gun powder and bullets attached to a five-gallon gas can that was thrown inside the building, through a window. The fire department could not get near the building since the office contained 300,000 rounds of ammunition stored inside.

Brian said, "Boss, we have been told that we are not to interfere in the FBI investigations, and if we received any info as to the whereabouts of these two, to immediately advise them."

"Of course, Brian."

"Pete, thank God no one got hurt, and we closed the office to make sure no one stayed behind because we felt that they were possibly up to something."

A press conference was held where I learned that the FBI was going to offer a reward of $25,000 for information leading to the arrest of these brothers. Once the FBI finished their briefing, I was asked to speak!

I informed the media that we were thankful, that none of our agents and staff were present when this bombing occurred. I thanked the FBI and all law enforcement and fire department help on this matter, and that I was advised by DEA Washington, it was also offering a $30,000 reward for any information as to the whereabouts of these individuals which would lead to their arrest and trial.

Within two days, we got a tip from a person in Orlando providing us the location of these brothers and where they were making phone calls from a pay phone around the corner of their hideout.

The brothers were quickly arrested by DEA Orlando agents. We could not wait for them to flee and ordered our Orlando agents to move in and arrest these individuals immediately on our call and later to turn them over to the FBI.

When an incident like this occurs, it becomes personal, and DEA has always responded with swift speed and with no holds barred. From experience with some FBI bosses, they do not share information, and this was Brian's call and mine alone, "Mission Accomplished!! We were not seeking publicity, just swift action!

Matthews cut a deal with the government and pleaded guilty to the bombing of the DEA Office and to the murder of a federal witness Stephen Franken and to running a drug beach ring from 1987 until March. He was charged also with possession with intent to distribute more than 11 pounds of cocaine and running a criminal enterprise. On October 1,1990, Jeffrey Matthews was sentenced to life imprisonment without possibility of parole. His brother's status is not available.

The estimated cost of the damage to our building was $4 million. This was a shocking experience which showed that because of our determination to put drug organizations out of business, that we had to always stay vigil.

Back at the office, Anita advised me that Stan the RAIC from our Gainesville Office was on the phone wanting to speak with me immediately!

"What's up, Stan?"

"Pete! We got a big problem!"

"Stan! Calm down. No problem is too big. You know me. I love challenges! Hit me!"

"Pete, we got a call from the Florida State Patrol for assistance on the turnpike. They stopped a Spanish male who possessed several hundred kilograms of cocaine in his car. I'm at the scene now and in interviewing him, he stated he was working for DEA as an informant for a DEA agent in one of our northern offices. He was to bring this shipment and deliver it to a major trafficker and this was his third shipment that he had picked up from Miami."

"Stan! Arrest this guy now, and I will make some calls immediately to that office to find out what the hell is going on, and why we weren't notified on this. This smells and sounds like we got a rogue agent!"

I immediately called this major office and spoke to the associate SAIC, who was a great friend of mine. I explained to him what we had and asked if he knew about this case. He responded, "I'll check, Frenchy. I know nothing about this. Give me the name of this informant to check his status. Hold on! Good God almighty, this guy has been paid numerous times by this agent, Pete! I'm on it now and the shit is about to hit the fan! Big time, pal!"

"Thanks, Pal, keep me posted!"

I learned that my friend had referred this matter to Internal Affairs who thoroughly investigated it. The agent thankfully was acting on his own to make a case and circumvented his superiors. That was an error on his part, and he paid the price for it!

Agents who refuse to be supervised and act on their own does not belong in DEA and need to be removed immediately. This work requires teamwork by all, and rogue agents, regardless of rank, are dangerous and need immediate removal.

The job of an ASAIC is very rewarding and demands a lot of interaction with all team members under his command. The responsibility rests on his shoulder and the RAIC's call their shots. I was there to assist when needed and not micromanage these bosses.

16
Tampa Resident Office
Operation Woodpecker

May 3, 1988

7,303 Pounds of Cocaine

Tampa Resident Office

W hen you read articles about South Florida in the 80s which made references that it is snowing in South Florida, this was not real snow! It was a casual term by law enforcement narcotic agencies made regarding the fact that the State of Florida was being inundated with cocaine.

Mike informed me that his office had gotten information that a shipment of cocaine had been off loaded in a warehouse in Tampa. The investigation was named "Operation Woodpecker" and the agents led by Mike resulted in the seizure of 7303 pound of cocaine, concealed in Cypress wood boards brought in from Brazil, South America. The boards were glued together with kilograms of cocaine concealed inside the square 15 ft board. The value of the cocaine was at $23,000 per kilo or about $167,969,000.

Seizures in those days were weekly occurrences.

17
Marijuana Indoor Grow Program Gulf Hydroponics

D EA initiated a program due to a nationwide increase of arrests and seizure of marijuana being grown indoors.

Tom Cash and Lionel met with me and advised me of this new DEA program and asked me to pick two agents to work for me on this operation. They said that because of my experience and knowledge of finding heroin laboratories in France, we could get results fast in training our people on the growing problem with these clandestine operations with some good agents.

I advised the bosses that I was honored to be picked and would get this going immediately.

The first thing I did was to target the Miami area. I immediately googled "Hydroponic indoor lights stores" and found one withing a mile of our office.

"Rita, get Ken McCarron, Tommy Davis (RIP), and ASAIC Al Coward on the phone for me and ask them to come to my office, please."

I heard Rita say, "He's waiting, and he is mad as hell! Be ready for it!"

"I heard you, Rita. Lunch is on you today," I responded while laughing. In no time, they were in my office. Al began, "Mr. Charette sir, pleasure to meet with you, I'm sure this is going to be good!"

Mac said, "I didn't do it, Frog, I plead the fifth!"

I admired these two agents, and we remain friends.

"It's getting deep in here; walk lightly both of you!" I began lightheartedly. "Sit down, close the door and Rita, unless it's the President, no calls, please."

I briefed them on this new program, telling them that I had to pick two agents to work under my supervision and train them on finding these clandestine locations. Cash told me to choose the best, and Mac was my choice. "Al, I want your support and please advise his supervisor that he is being detailed to me and get one more agent to work with Mac on this. I will brief you every day on the progress. I know the supervisor will be upset, but if he wishes to discuss this matter with you and me, I will gladly meet with him."

Mac blurted, "Oh shit, the Frog is loose."

"Al, Pete, you got it. I will inform him with pleasure. Anything else, you're welcome to go with us tomorrow on our first training day. I guarantee that we will have our first target before the end of the day." Al left and Mac stayed behind.

"I don't know what to say, Pete! Thank you for this opportunity, and I won't let you down."

"Mac, I've watched you since I have been here and admire your tenacity to get results on cases and have no doubt you and Tommy will shine. Mac You will oversee this operation. You are the best in this division. So, let's kick ass!"

The feedback I got was that the supervisor was not a happy camper!

Mac did not waste time and bought himself a High Times magazine which was all about marijuana. He did his research and found a supply store named Gulf Coast Hydroponics in Miami located on Byrd Road. The owner of the store was Mike Ulla. Upon entering, he heard music "Bad Moon Rising" by Creedence Clearwater on the store speakers. Mac started singing the song to himself and loud enough to be heard by the three store owners.

The agents from his group set up a surveillance team on the

store while Mac went in the store wearing a hidden microphone. The Suspect Ulla greeted Mac saying that he liked his singing voice and asked how he could help him. Mac informed him that he was interested in setting up a hydroponic grow house and asked how this could be done and what he needed to start this. He was shown the merchandise needed to do this, and Mac informed him that he had to rent a warehouse first and would be back and left.

Mac came back to the office and briefed me stating that the cost to set up this would be $7,000. I told him great work and to fill out a request form for my signature to get the money, and I'd sign it immediately.

He then returned to the store with a six pack of beer and asked the owner if he could do the installation for this operation. He then asked Mac to come with him to his office where they could talk in private. Once in the office, they sat down, and Mike and he had a beer. Mac informed him that he could set up his warehouse with no problem! "I need to know upfront, "Are you working for the cops? I've done eight years in prison in NY for shooting someone and ain't about to get arrested again!"

"No! Are you nuts?"

"Just being careful!"

"Okay! Can you do it?"

"I'm your man! Mike reached down and opened a desk drawer and pulled out a plastic clear bag, full of large marijuana buds and asking, "You want to do a joint together?"

Mac responded, "No way, my man! I was in Nam and that shit stoned me out, and I ended up shooting a soldier in my barrack! I got to drive and meet the warehouse owner to sign my rental contract."

Mac agreed on starting this right away, paid Mike the $7K on the spot and gave him the location of the warehouse to meet and bring all the hydroponic lamps and water system hoses, etc. and start the operation, the sooner the better. The entire setup was completed in a few days.

Once completed, Mike provided all the chemicals needed as well as the marijuana seeds which were planted.

Tom had informed Director Jack Lawn of this Operation "Gulf Coast Hydroponics," and Lawn came to Miami to see this undercover grow house.

The entire investigation lasted a couple of weeks and arrests were made, our first operation being a total success.

Surveillance continued to be done at the store identifying suspected growers who were purchasing indoor grow equipment and surveillance of these suspects' residences in the Miami area and Broward County areas.

The following steps were utilized in the preparation of getting probable cause for each warrant of this suspected residence:

Step One

Initiate surveillance on the hydroponic store, watch the clientele going in and out of the store, noting time, car model, tag number, and if carrying lighting goods, follow suspect from a distance to the residential residence and watch offloading the material purchased into the house. We waited approximately 20 minutes, and the suspect departed the store and was followed to his residence.

Step Two

Get utility records of electric service usage for three months, determine the lowest usage and compare the start of highest usage and show patterns on power usage. Grow lighting systems use excessive power since lighting is on for 24 hours daily. Same with Water Authority since marijuana growth requires extensive watering.

Step Three

Check windows of front and back and sides to see if they are boarded up. Photograph from outside shaded windows or boarded windows, conduct early surveillance of residence for activity going in and out and follow new suspects.

We requested from our technical division in Washington to immediately send us, the thermal gun for which we were lucky because there was only one left. This gun was used for aircraft surveillance and stationary surveillance to determine heat being dispersed throughout the residence that was abnormal and showed up as bright reddish yellow, giving additional probable cause for a search warrant. This residence heat glowed on the thermal gun on all rooms in the house and the roof being suspected of having indoor growth operation.

After two weeks of surveillance, we had sufficient probable cause for a search warrant which was then obtained.

This was our first operation of many to come. Mac decided to go undercover at the store as a client wishing to set up a grow operation. Mac was foaming at the mouth and proposed to go undercover at the hydroponic store and pose as a new, interested grower who wished to speak with the owner about starting his own grow operation.

This resulted in the arrest of the owner of the store and others. In a period of several months, our division seized 20 grow houses in the Broward and Dade Counties. Mac and his team had great success! Agents from other groups started making cases like this after seeing this success.

I have to say that I miss this very much!

18
Disgruntled Supervisor

Rita said, "Pete, Mac is here to see you!"

"Okay! Come in, Dog! Mind if I shut the door? He looked very down. "Mac, what's wrong, Pal? Are you ok?"

"Frog, look at this. Here, I just got my yearly evaluation from my GS, He rated me 'Minimally Satisfactory!' Frog, this is wrong, I busted my ass for one year on this operation. We made more seizures than any office in the U.S., and this is what he does to me because he resents you, and the fact that we are best friends outside of work! Frog, I've never used our friendship to advance myself. I do it on my own. You taught me that! "

"Mac, I know and never showed favoritism to you especially! Go back to your office. I'll handle this myself immediately!"

Mac left smiling, and I asked Anita to get Mac's GS to my office immediately.

Mac's supervisor walked in and shut the door. "You want to see me?"

"Yes, I do. Sit down. I've received information that rumors are being spread that you gave Agent McCarron a "Minimally Satisfactory" in his yearly evaluation. Is that correct!"

"Yeah! What about it?"

"I just wanted you to know that this is a personal issue. You did this because I used him on the Marijuana Grow Operation in which he took down over 20 grow operations in this state. I know through rumors that you hate my guts, which I really don't care about, but because of my friendship off the job, you stooped to the lowest to downgrade Mac, that's a cowardly act!

If you have a hatred for me, then I suggest you address it with me directly, You and I both come from the old school, and I distinctly remember that when there were issues between agents, they went out in the parking lot and settled it on the spot! I am game, are you?"

"Are you threatening me? "

"No, I'm telling you to think this over! Have a good day. Now get out of my sight! You need to review the evaluation of this great agent who isn't a coward like you!"

The subject was red face and left. Within 15 minutes, I got a call from Tom to come to his office. I knew that this supervisor was at Tom's office.

I walked into his office. "Yes Tom!"

"Have a seat. You know this person?"

"Yes, very well!"

"He has advised me that you threatened him. Is this correct?"

"Tom, no that's not correct. I gave him an education on how in the old days, if someone disliked you, then both parties would go outside and settle the issue in the parking lot!"

"What's the issue?" he asked beginning to smile.

"It involves Agent Ken McCarron (AKA aka "Big Dog"). This man gave him a poor rating, and rumors were brought to my attention that it was done purposely because Mac is a friend of mine off the job, and this person hates my guts, so this was done intentionally."

Tom turned to him and said, "You better reconsider this seriously."

The subject agreed, and within one hour Agent McCarron's evaluation was rated "Outstanding!"

This supervisor eventually requested a transfer to the West Coast and resigned from DEA. End of this matter.

Unfortunately, some supervisors in those days would use their dislike of some agents to attempt to ruin their careers and weren't professional enough to realize that this should not have any bearing on them. I understand some people did not like my presence as an agent. "I excelled on my own merits, doing my job, without trying to kiss ass and made sure that I always stood firm. Back in my office, I was advised that my ASAIC friend Charles Lutz had received a transfer notice to go too Headquarters, DC. Chuck was a great friend and still is.

Tom Cash had to rearrange some positions and advised me and the rest of our team, that I was being transferred to be the new ASAIC of The Caribbean Country offices which included Freeport, Nassau, Port Au Prince, Santa Domingo, Kingston, Barbados, and Miami Group 10 International Group. In addition, the three foreign county Attachés' Inspectors from the Canadian RCMP, the French Narcotic Police Judiciary, and the German Bundist Criminalist Narcotic Bureau would work under me.

19
Change of Assignment
ASAIC Miami Country Offices
5-12-1990 To 12-19-1993

U nfortunately, I had to go to my new office on the first floor
and had a new secretary named Norma. Rita was the best
and was devastated not to be assigned to my new position
for which I tried to keep her but to no avail.

I settled in, and Norma briefed me on the daily operations
of the division. She advised me that all the field secretaries were
instructed that they must go through her if they needed to talk to
me. I was struck by that and said to her, "Norma, I work differently
than some bosses as you will learn. My policy is that anyone who
wants to speak to me directly can do so anytime! I have an open-
door policy, and you and I will work great together.

"Mr. Charette, I fully understand. I'm just used to the previous
bosses who required that we follow that system."

Laughing and shaking my head I said, "Norma, you did what
they asked you to do, but I am a simple man, no better than anyone
else, as you will see, and I appreciate your professionalism, and it
will please me very much if you call me Pete from here on. We
will work great together, trust me! I appreciate your briefing me.
Can you call John Brown to come to my office if he is not tied
up?"

"Will do, Pete. God, that feels good already!" She let out a
sigh of relief.

"Now you're talking!"

My door was kept open, and I heard JB's voice as he walked in, smiling broadly! "Pete! You son of a gun!" We shook hands and embraced each other with a big hug.

"JB! Look at you! If someone would have said to us in agent school that we would be together again like this, I would have told them bullshit."

From day one when we first met, we connected immediately, and it was a lifetime friendship! Our meeting lasted an hour, and John had the best group of agents in the Miami Field Division and the best secretary in the division named Suzan Ramirez who was loved by everyone in the group including myself.

I told JB, that this was his group, and I knew that he and his group were top case makers, and I was anxious to meet them.

"Norma, I'm going to group 10 to meet the group, and go ahead to lunch. I will be at lunch with the group. Lunch breaks with me are one hour.

Entering the Group 10 office, I was greeted by Suzy who said, "Welcome and glad to have you as our boss!"

"Thanks, Suzy! Glad to be here also!"

JB began, "Listen up, guys. Let's circle around with our chairs. Pete is here to meet you all."

"Frog, it's your show!"

"Guys, as I looked around the last time, I saw most of you were at the old building when I became one of you and shipped off to France in 1972 and now came back 10 years later!

JB and I were in the same BNDD class in D.C., and here we are together again! The scary thing is we think alike, we do kick ass.

"I expect that all of you are case makers and since you're assigned to the Caribbean Division, you are also our representatives with our foreign counterparts. I've discussed with JB that he assigns you all as partners and that you will be expected to do liaison visits to our country offices and police units at various islands at least quarterly and offer to do joint cases together. I know that this was not being done through no fault of this group, but rest assured it's going to be a requirement. JB and I will travel also to our country office's and get them on board and to refer cases to you that needs work stateside. I see some of you are already smiling! I'm a fanatic when it comes to doing liaison with police departments worldwide, and trust me, the result is fantastic. Also, when you do your liaison, you will be given a liaison entertainment fund for your visit!

"All we expect is a report in writing as with whom you met, name, title, and suggestions.

Domestically here in Miami, you can work cases. Also, we have no boundaries. One last thing is that we be safe and always remember 'If anyone must die, it's not you, it's them.'"

John's team members were Kenny Peterson, Ken McCarron, Gene Francar, Pete Serron, Tommy Golden, Kevin O'Brien, Valerie Gibson, Drew Lasker, Kevin Stevens, Steve Murphy of (TV Star Narco)

It was time now for my going to visit our country offices, to meet the host country's narcotic directors, be briefed, and to meet our agents.

The first office was our Nassau Office which had a major impact on drug smuggling from Colombia by aircraft doing air drops of bails of cocaine into the Caribbean waters to awaiting go-fast Donzi Boats who picked up the floating bails and brought them in to the East Coast areas of Miami, Ft. Lauderdale and delivered to stash houses along the Inter-coastal Waterway and canal residences. The average shipments were approximately 350 kilograms (551.16 lbs.).

The office had 10 agents and had a major program ongoing 24 hours a day called Operation Bahama and Turk. This was an air interdiction program which used sensitive aerostat blimps and radar balloons located on several islands and which picked up tracking of planes flying out of suspected airfields of the shores of

Colombia. This involved a complex network of radar tracking and of flight patterns that suspected planes used to fly to the Bahamas. The gathered intelligence was helpful in selecting a bogey and tracking the flight pattern and estimating flight to the Bahamas.

Once confirmed as target, OPBAT Command Center at our DEA Office scrambled the team of agents which consisted of DEA agents, Bahamian Defense Force, narcotic agents, and United States Black Hawk helicopters and the U.S. Coast Guard team who had been tasked to proceed in the direction of the suspected air drop. Notified immediately was our partner the U.S. Customs Air Wing Pilots who flew toward the target in a private jet and got behind the target to follow it to the Bahamian waters where our team was concealed on nearby Islands. Once the signal was given by the Customs pilot that the bogey was dropping altitude and circling an awaiting boat for pick up and dropping the bails out of an open door into the sea, the move signal was then given to the Black Hawk chopper captain at the time of sighting to move on the boat that was loaded with the bails of cocaine. The boat would usually try to outrun the helicopter and head for the Cuban DMZ Zone for safe entry there.

If the bogey refused to stop, quite often the suspected driver and aid would give us the index finger sign and refuse to stop. The command was given to put several machine-gun shots across the bow of the boat and if they didn't comply, to put a 50-caliber shot into the engine so he would not make it to the DMZ Zone. Thousands of kilograms were lost because we were forbidden to cross the DMZ line or communicate with the Colombian authorities. The only ones permitted to do this was the U.S. Coast Guard.

I had a meeting with the Country Attaché John Pully and the U.S. Ambassador Chic HEEK, who was a great Ambassador and friend of DEA. I learned about the frustration of being unable to pursue and hand off the bogeys to the Cuban authorities because of our State Department orders. My personal feelings and that of our agents were that it was bull shit. I voiced my view to Tom Cash on this matter who advised that he felt the same way, but the State Department in Washington called the shots on Foreign Affairs! The President at that time was 'Slick Willy' as we called him Clinton who opposed our enforcement actions with the use of aerostat blimps. He eventually removed the Blimp Radar system from the program.

20
Enough Is Enough
The Hell with Politics

On August 19, 1993, I received a phone call from John in Nassau that was urgent.

"Pete, I'm fed up with us not having authority to pursue a load of cocaine into Cuba. Enough is enough! This is bull shit! We have a boat being pursued, and I want you to authorize us, to go all the way and allow me to communicate directly with the Cuban authorities on this chase and hand them over to their Coast Guard."

"John, I am just as frustrated as you, and I'm ready to take the hit on this. Tell your team it's a green light and make your call and coordinate with them on this. I'm behind you and the guys, and we can bring this to a head once and for all! Keep me posted, and I'll tell Cash and make sure you tell Chic ASAP!!"

"Thanks' Pete!"

There comes a time when doing this job that if you are in command and are not willing to take a chance, you need to step down because you have failed your agents because of stupid policies that should have been reviewed and updated a long time before this!

Cash and I met, and he immediately notified the Director Robert Bonner who supported our action and stood behind us 100% without hesitation.

The two smugglers identified as Jorge Lam, 33, and Jose

Clemente, 31, from Sweetwater, Florida were confined in Cuba and for the first time notified us that the suspects were being turned over to us. The pickup was made, and a DEA private jet with John Pully and U.S. Marshalls brought them to Miami for prosecution in the U.S.

Defendants L/R: ASAIC Pierre Charette, Jorge Lam, Jose Clemente and Press Agent MFD James Shedd

Their speedboat the, Thief of Hearts, was also surrendered to DEA on the high seas by the Cuban Coast Guard. The case represented that this was first time Cuban authorities have returned a boat and its evidence and violators to the United States.

Director Bonner announced that the "The Cooperation provided by the Cuban authorities in this case is an important step forward in our bilateral counter-narcotics relationship."

The shipment of cocaine was 325 kilograms (Value $7,150,00

@ $22K per kilo).

John Pully and the entire team were praised for taking this risky action that opened direct communication with Cuba on Narcotic investigations.

DEA always has found ways to communicate with our foreign counterparts, and I firmly agree that politics should not interfere with this serious job. This decision proves that there are no boundaries to narcotic enforcement. Diplomatic courtesy is good and should be followed up to a certain point. When it comes to preventing drug use and drug trafficking, then ensure that people's rights are protected. But trafficking and selling illegal drugs are an open invitation to us to use whatever legal means we have, and results like this prove that we need to do our job and for others to stay out of our way.

The Nassau country office deserves praise for their dedication to the OPBAT Program during my last year. The total amount of cocaine seized in one year was 55,000 pounds of cocaine valued at 110 million dollars.

21
Dominican Republic
Santa Domingo
1991

I visited all our country offices, and the team meetings resulted in a great work atmosphere, which already was in place with few changes made. Two cases that made quite an impact needs to be part of this account and which were eye openers!

Our office in Santa Domingo became a new route for attempts by the Colombian Cartel to use the Dominican Republic as an offloading of cocaine shipments destined for Florida and for the cartel's money laundering.

Our office in Santa Domingo was a two-man office. The country attaché was Victor Oliveri, and the agent was Fidel Sanchez. I visited their office with the new Deputy Assistant Agent in Charge Frank Tarallo (aka "The Don'") to all his friends. Frank and I worked in Europe where he was Country attaché in Rome. Frank was a close friend and one of the best undercover agents in the FBN and BNDD. I had advised him on my travels to this office, and he accompanied me to meet with the ambassador of the embassy to meet the head of the Dominican Narcotics Bureau.

Upon arrival, we were greeted by Victor and Fidel at the airport, flown there on our DEA airplane by the head of the DEA Air Wing based at Opa-Locka Airport in Miami along with his copilot Mike Price.

From there we were going to our Barbados, Kingston, and Jamaica Offices.

Once checked into our hotel, we went to the Embassy to meet the ambassador and had a one-hour meeting with him.

After discussing the drug situation that impacted the U.S. from traffickers of Santa Domingo, we were taken to the hotel for a meeting with the head of the Narcotic Bureau Captain Julio Caesar Ventura Bayonet the next morning. Fidel took us to the Hotel Bar and had a few beers with us and discussed a case that he had just finished working in May 1991 with our office in Colombia were a CI pilot from Colombia flew in 750 kilograms undercover to a small airstrip outside Santa Domingo. The pilot was given $50,000 to fly the load, and an undercover police officer was given $10,000 for protecting the area. After several meetings occurred, the plane came in with 750 kilograms of cocaine and 6 persons were arrested. The cocaine was seized along with the plane. This was a joint operation with the Narcotic Bureau headed by a general whom we did not meet for reasons that cannot be disclosed. The second in command was Captain Bayonet. We could tell by his enthusiasm that Fidel was the one who kept the liaison strong at this office.

The next day we met with Bayonet and met his Investigators who presented us with a thorough briefing. We agreed on meeting later after supper with Fidel and his family. Fidel explained to us that there was turmoil with the drug unit and alleged corruption by the head of the unit. He advised that he wanted us to meet with Bayonet and have a meeting with a special person whose medical office was nicknamed "El Doctore" in the community and was a trusted friend of the president. Once a week on Tuesdays the doctor had poor families come to his home and receive free medical aid, all night long. He was loved by the community and was a very close friend of Fidel.

After supper, we met with Capitan Bayonet and drove to meet the doctor. Upon arriving at his residence, we observed a line of families that almost circled the entire block. It was a scene out of a movie, and we were immediately escorted to meet the doctor in his living room. Introductions were made, and he welcomed us and advised that he wanted us to know that Fidel was highly regarded by the president and Captain Bayonet and his very effective team of investigators. He expressed to us that he was concerned about the general in charge and had advised his friend the president, that due to alleged suspicions being discussed by influential people in high places in the government about his possible affiliations with questionable drug traffickers, that he needed to be transferred out of this position. Captain Bayonet was honest, displayed great integrity and was fully endorsed by DEA for a promotion to be in charge.

He advised us that he had communicated this to President Balaguer's niece, who was his advisor, and that she was waiting for us to meet with her now at the Presidential Palace. We thanked him for this meeting, and we were transported to the palace to meet with her discreetly. We expressed to her our concerns about the selection of the head of this country's narcotic bureau, and that we would like to see Captain Bayonet whom we highly trusted to work closely with him and his investigators. She totally agreed with us and appreciated our relationship with her uncle's government. She further conveyed her uncle's message to us but due to health problems, he regretted not being available to meet us. She would convey our support and considerations for Captain Bayonet being promoted to this office. Our meeting was extremely cordial, and we were assured that this matter would be a high priority matter and resolved quickly.

We returned to our hotel. Captain Bayonet was very thankful for our support and would meet with us at his office tomorrow. Fidel advised us that word spreads around quickly and wouldn't be surprised if the Ambassador received a call on our secret meeting.

The next morning, we went to the DEA office where Victor advised us that the ambassador wanted to meet with us about our meeting of last night. We met with the ambassador who advised us that he had received a call by a source who advised him of our visit with Balaguer's niece and asked for details. Frank advised him that we had been asked to meet with the doctor about a serious concern regarding the current general in charge of the narcotic bureau, and after meeting with him, he advised us that the niece of the president wanted to meet with us, which had been arranged quietly.

The ambassador thanked us for briefing him and wished us safe travel. Victor was briefed and thanked us for supporting Bayonet after which we all went and met with him and thanked him for supporting us and the United States on our war on drugs. We learned that morning that the president made an announcement that Captain Bayonet was promoted to general and placed in charge of the Narcotic Division while the current general was moved to a different position. This was great news and Fidel was overwhelmed with joy over the news.

We went to the airport where Joe met us and off we flew to Barbados to visit our office. The visit went extremely well, and we returned to Miami two days later.

Caption: Right to left- Agent Fidel Sanchez, Deputy SAIC Frank Tarallo, General Bayonet, ASAIC Pierre Charette, Country Attaché Victor Sanchez.

22

Money Laundering and Implication of the Colombian Counsel General of Montevideo, Uruguay

November 1992

A gent Fidel Sanchez had been requested to work undercover for the Buenos Aires DEA office who had a confidential source that had been approached by the Colombian Counsel General in Montevideo named Gustava Pastrana. He was a cousin related to Andres Pastrana, who was running for President of Colombia. The source told DEA that Gustava was doing money laundering, and the source was told to tell Gustava that he has a client in Miami that needed to launder $250,000 and Gustava agreed to fly in Miami with the CI to meet this person. The meeting was arranged by Agent Sanchez, and our Caribbean Group 10 arranged for a meeting in Miami. Agent Fidel Sanchez arranged with our Caribbean Group 10 to have the meeting take place on a DEA undercover boat, captained by DEA Undercover Agent Gill Charette (my brother).

Sanchez met with Gustava on the boat which was wired to tape all conversations. The meeting was held, and details of this suspect's money laundering operation were discussed. Special Agent Sanchez agreed to have him launder $250,000 which he gave to him and provided details of where to wire the money to a false account in the Philippines which had been established by

DEA. The funds arrived in two days.

A second meeting occurred in December with Gustava. He mentioned that he had spoken with his cousin about this first transaction, and his cousin asked him to get a campaign contribution from Fidel. He was given another $250,000 during which Group 10 Agents who were surveilling this meeting moved in and arrested Gustava. When arrested, Gustava was carrying a briefcase which was seized, and which contained money and photographs of him and his cousin at a campaign appearance. His cousin was elected President of Colombia. This photo was sent to Washington and indicated that corruption had worked its way to the top of the government of Colombia.

Photo Seized at time of arrest Gustava and Cousin who became President of Colombia. Gustava was charged with money laundering in the Southern District and convicted to 10 years in federal prison in November of 1992.

23
Radio Telecommunication Intercept
Santo Domingo, Dominican Republic
November 1992

Through a great joint relationship with General Bayonet and his drug unit, a radio listening operation named Operation Omega was established to monitor any possible aircraft communication originating out of Colombia to the Dominican Republic. In early March 1992, aircraft communication intercepted a possible suspect plane which had communicated arrival time at a small air strip located 60 miles from Santa Domingo, estimated arrival time at 4 a.m. DEA Agent Fidel Sanchez coordinated with the OPBAT the helicopter unit to have a team with the Dominican narcotic investigator and DEA OPBAT team along with a ground surveillance team to effect an arrest once the aircraft had landed and began offloading the cocaine cargo.

The aircraft, a twin-engine King Air, landed and the ground team gave the signal for the Black Hawk military OPBAT team to land and surround the area and arrest the three suspects on the plane. They then seized the plane and confiscated 50 kilograms (110 pounds) of cocaine valued at $53,724,00. One of the suspects attempted to run with an attaché case, containing $50,000.

24
Group 10
Caribbean International Group

roup 10 was supervised by John Brown (aka "JB") when I assumed this division, followed by Supervisor Dick Stuart. Both were by far the best in the Miami Field Division. To be more specific, they kicked ass!

The Agents were Top Row–Gene Francar (aka "Gino"), Supervisor John Brown, Kenny Peterson, ASAIC Pete Charette, Pete Saron, Tommy Golden, Kevin Obrien, Valerie Gibson, Drew Lasker. Bottom Row–Kevin Stephen, Steve Murphy (aka "NARCO"). All of them were from the old BNDD day, and the best!

Case photo is case developed by Agent Drew Lasker and

Thomas Golden, seizure of 1000 kilos of cocaine on 07-26-1990 in Key Biscayne, FL. (Value $ 22 Million)

Cash seizure of $765,000

ASAIC Pierre Charette

Returning from lunch, Group 10 agents observed suspicious individuals loading boxes of air conditioning units into a truck from an appliance store one block away from our office. Agents from Group 10 converged on these very nervous and suspicious individuals and stopped them, got consent to open boxes, and seized $765,000 of drug money.

SAIC Thomas Cash, 12-14-1990
Vega Baya, Puerto Rico $13,800,000

Search Warrant seizure of drug smuggler retirement funds found hidden behind walls in the defendant's residence in Puerto Rico.

Throughout my career I have worked with some of the most outstanding private citizens' confidential sources worldwide. One of them was an ex-Deputy Sheriff from Alabama Edward Geiman (aka "Fast Eddie"), whom I met in 1970 when I was a narcotics agent in the Broward County Sheriff's Department in Ft. Lauderdale. He had a great talent and conviction to work with law enforcement agencies in an undercover capacity. Over the years, he was responsible for the introduction of numerous state and federal agents in the arrest of numerous violators involved in trafficking large quantities of narcotics throughout the South, Florida and other states. On many occasions he risked his life to assist law enforcement and was always arrested with the violators to maintain his cover. Ed's passion was always to work with law enforcement and infiltrate himself into the criminal underworld to rid society of these animals. We have remained friends ever since 1970. Persons like him are far and few and deserve recognition for their service. He helped our group 10 on several occasions, resulting in arrests and seizures of cocaine.

Group 10 Operation Cornerstone, 1991
Seizure 12,250 kilograms of cocaine, value - $ 269.5 million

This case was unique in nature. DEA Miami Field Division had received from a source, that the Colombian Cartel had a shipment of cocaine stored in an open lot in the Miami area inside a concrete post. The source could not give any additional information as to the location.

Group 10 Supervisor and Agent Tommy Golden had gone to lunch with Frank Tarallo and me and returning to the office, S/A Golden observed this concrete post behind a chain linked fence on the left side of the street and said, "I wonder if this is the alert shipment we received today." Group 10 was teamed up and set up surveillance on this lot. This paid off when several flatbed trailers backed up to the posts and loaded them up on the trucks. Suspects in sedans acted as lookouts and the trucks, escorted by the cars, left and headed towards West Palm Beach to a warehouse. A total of 2430 concrete posts were contained in the shipment. The team apprehended the suspects. Concealed inside each of the hollowed posts were 6 kilograms of cocaine. Total weight of the seizure was 12, 250 kilograms of cocaine. This was one of the largest seizures of cocaine made at that time.

There was never a dull moment during my assignment to the Caribbean Division. The entire offices were always busy, and we had great cooperation from all our foreign counterparts.

While I was at my desk, Norma advised me that there were two visitors wishing to meet with me at the front desk. She returned to the front desk and escorted them to the conference room where I was waiting.

12, 250 kilograms of cocaine concealed in cement post.
Value - $428,750,000

I stood up and greeted these two well-dressed gentlemen who introduced themselves hereafter with the code names "Miguel and Rudolph." These two professional businessmen advised me that they had read about me in the newspaper and had decided that I was the man they wanted to share their story with about their association with the Colombian Cartel drug kingpins. They advised me that they had lost family members including nieces and nephews to the drugs being supplied to the U.S. by the cartel and now were prepared have these criminals arrested. They advised that they were closely associated with Pablo Escobar and his organization and had attended many social parties at their residences.

I had Supervisor John Brown and Ken Peterson join us and turned them over to them for a complete debriefing and assured them that we would be honored to have their help in this matter. We ended up confiscating numerous deliveries and seizures of cocaine through their efforts. In addition, at my request I asked them to travel to Colombia and that I needed direct proof that

Escobar's cartel was rumored to set up heroin laboratories, and we needed to prove to Washington that this in effect was true. They advised me that they would get on this immediately.

Washington Heroin Division had been receiving our intelligence on this and doubted them, but I was determined to prove them wrong with pictures of poppy fields, heroin samples, and documents of their travels and pictures, etc.

After being in Colombia for several weeks and talking with us on a special secured satellite phone, they notified us that they had what we suspected and were bringing samples and an alarming new method of deception to bring in the heroin. They asked for us to meet them at U.S. Customs to clear them through with samples they were bringing in.

I advised Tom Cash who was anxious to see what they had. I told Tom that those in D.C. doubted us, and I would be honored to do the presentation in person and have them with me with their proof and testimony

We cleared them through customs after which they came to the office for a debriefing. Rudolph had already written their reports and activities and had picture proof of the poppy fields and coordinates for satellite photography to be done.

The unbelievable surprise was when Miguel said, "Boss, here is the shocker," and pulled out a plastic toy. "Boss, this is heroin, disguised as a toy vehicle! Take it to your lab and have them heat dissolve it and separate the plastic and other liquid then process it into a powder solution. You will conclude that it will be heroin!" We took it to the lab director, and we were blown away! When it was analyzed, it was separated and tested positive for heroin!

It was shocking that this process could be used in the disguised form of toys and any other plastic forms without detection. Our lab people were shocked at this new process.

I went to D.C. HQ and presented the findings with our professional sources bringing about some red faces of those who did not like being proven wrong. We walked out smiling from ear to ear!

These two professionals wrote the best intelligence reports I had ever seen.

One of the requests we had for these two was for the agency for intelligence to contact Tom Cash for debriefing. Tom had me come to his office and told me of the request. I told him no because they were our source (Group 10), and no one will ever have that opportunity except us. They made it very clear to me that they speak to no one except me and Group 10. Tom advised them that I refused to make the two available to them; However, Tom honored my request, but now was on their shit list!

A new agent assigned to Group 10 was Agent Peter Scrocca, Jr., son of retired GS Pete Scrocca (deceased), one of the most respected and loved GS in FBN/ BNDD/ DEA. Young Peter had a tough battle to overcome his dad's willingness to help become a great agent. I remember interviewing him when he was selected. Pete called me and said his son was coming in to be interviewed and asked if I could sit on the interview board. Without hesitation, I told him to consider it done.

Peter Junior came in for the interview nervous as hell. The board had decided to put him through the grinder, but the bottom line was that he was quite capable to do this successfully without good old dad!

The interview lasted an hour while messing with him, and then we asked him to step outside during which we would vote and call him back shortly. We all laughed, since he was exhausted from nerves, especially when he was asked, "Does Dad always step in for you? We received a call from him telling us you were a good son and would make a great agent!" His shoulders drooped, and you could tell that dad's interference was a kiss of death! It was hard to keep a straight face.

Finally, we called him back. He sat down, and we told him that we had a problem. He immediately froze up tight, and we told him that if Dad was going to interfere with work, that we couldn't hire someone for that reason. Shelled shocked, he looked as if he was going to pass out! I told him, "Peter, your dad did what any of us would do! Congratulations, Peter! We all agreed that you will be an outstanding agent! Welcome aboard!"

He had the biggest smile and thanked all of us. I told him to call his dad because he was probably in a panic by now. We all laughed.

Young Peter, after 12 weeks of agent school, received his appointment orders that he was being assigned to the Miami Field Division. Sure, enough, I got a call from Big Pete, and before he could say anything, I said, "Keep your mouth shut, and listen to me. Yes, he's coming to Miami and Cash agreed to have him in my Group 10 International group. Pete, He can do it on his own! You helped me, and I never forgot that! You owe the Cheech and me a few drinks, and you're paying for the entire Friday bill at the airport watering hole. Pay back is hell, Mr. Scrocca. I haven't forgotten that you did the same thing to me with Ben and Miller and the guys when we celebrated my being hired!"

"You SOB! You still remember that don't you?" "Yep!"

Young Peter's first case was made by him and his dad's old informant, which resulted in one of the biggest indoor operations in Homestead, Florida. While arresting the owner of the marijuana hydroponic farm, we observed across the street parked in front of the house Mom and Dad, watching it all happen. Peter Senior had to be there for his son's first takedown! I would have done the same!

Peter, Jr. became an outstanding Agent and became the Head of Internal Affair for the Miami Field Division and remains a great friend!

Seizure Indoor Grow. Homestead, FL
L/R ASAIC Charette, Agent 's Ken McCarron, Jim Nimms, Peter Scrocca Jr.,
Rick Bendakovick.

25
Time to Retire
12-19-1993

I came home Dec 1,1993, and my wife Janice looked at me and said, "Oh God! What's Up? You have that look and grin!"

"Guess what I did today? I have given my two weeks' notice, and I'm retiring effective December 19, 1993."

"Are you serious? Why?"

"Janice, I caught one of our inspectors from D.C. in the hallway of the building and asked him how he was doing, and he said, "Pete, great. Look, I know we must report to you ASAICs or Tom if we come in on an allegation, per Trooper One Orders (Administrators' nickname by agents). Pete, he sent us here to investigate an agent for using a government car to stop at a 7-Eleven store to purchase a gallon of milk on his way home! A citizen reported this to Trooper One.

"You got to be kidding me! He violated his own order by telling you not to check in with us. This is bullshit, and this guy is wrong. This agency is not the agency that I signed up for, and it's time to pack it in! Let's go see Tom!"

Tom was shocked. I left and went to see our Administrative Officer who checked and said that with my military time, I was eligible to retire now at 50 years of age, and I would not gain any more money by staying to 57 years of age, which is mandatory. I told her to get the paperwork done and bring it to me to sign. I'll give you two weeks' notice and advise Tom."

Tom accepted my notice and agreed that things weren't the same anymore and hated to see me go.

I had the most fantastic career that an agent could have had. I made the best friends and from 1963-1993, it was the greatest ride that a law enforcement officer could have had. I accomplished my goals in putting violators in prison, and I made it to the top of the drug chain as planned.

My memories will be there forever for having worked side by side with the greatest agents in the world!

God Bless law enforcement and all of my agent brothers and sisters

PART TWO

OPERATION SOUTHERN COMFORT

1
Rosenthal, Largest Cocaine Conspiracy in United States' History
January 26, 1982- January 22,1984

The Attorney General of the United States proclaimed this incredible case as the "Largest Cocaine Ring ever discovered in U.S. history." The Conspiracy Indictment unsealed charged 55 persons with smuggling $3.8 billion worth of cocaine into the United States.

This conspiracy was headed up by Harold Rosenthal who was ranked as #15 on the FBI's most wanted federal fugitive.

This case was filled with intrigue, killings, prison escapes, and drug trafficking by Colombia's famous worldwide drug lord Pablo Escobar and Harold Rosenthal.

Harold Rosenthal was the U.S. mob's broker for cocaine shipments through Escobar and was protected in Medellin, Colombia from being extradited to the U.S. He was involved in the plan to kill the Attorney General of Colombia, Laura Bonnilla.

According to the Atlanta police, he was "a cop's dream; he was considered a big time criminal, and it would have been a feather in their cap to capture him."

(Source: *Atlanta Journal* staff writer Sam Hopkins, staff writer 9/1/83)

U.S. Department of Justice Wanted Poster Harold Rosenthal

Rosenthal's drug organization successfully shipped into the U.S. over 8,050 kilos of cocaine during a period of two years. Based on intelligence information, in 1982 Rosenthal was responsible for 60% of all the cocaine imported to the U.S. It was estimated that the volume by the group far exceeded the loads documented in the indictment and may well have reached over 100,000 pounds (50 tons). Rosenthal's smuggling operation was worth $5.1 billion.

There were also orders to kill the DEA undercover pilot and the attorney general of Colombia by Escobar's organization which was faked and planned.

On January 26, 1982, while sitting at my desk, Agent Mona Polen asked to speak with me about interviewing a confidential source with Agent Bennie Swint, referred to them by a U.S. Marshall in Atlanta, regarding federal fugitive Harold Joseph Rosenthal and associate Leonard Bonnel Steele and others. The interview took place at our office, and the source indicated knowing the whereabouts of Rosenthal and of his ongoing drug smuggling operation.

The source advised of having been a member of Rosenthal's smuggling organization and had known Rosenthal for approximately 25 years when Rosenthal had a bond business in Atlanta. Rosenthal at that time had introduced Leonard Steele to the source, who was a City of Atlanta Bond Clerk, and later moved to Ft. Lauderdale.

At that time in 1976/1977, the source became involved in drug smuggling of cocaine to the U.S. with them. Rosenthal told the source that he needed a passport and to get one for him to travel to Colombia concerning a false equipment deal. The trip lasted one month, and the source learned that Rosenthal was arranging cocaine connections for his smuggling operation.

When they returned, Rosenthal smuggled one pound of cocaine strapped to his body. A second trip was made two months later, and meetings were arranged to meet two suppliers of cocaine. Rosenthal purchased a DC-3 aircraft for his smuggling operation. The source learned at that time about Rosenthal's large scale cocaine drug smuggling operation and sale of guns. He was arrested for cocaine trafficking in Atlanta in 1981 and sentenced to 31 years in federal prison. He escaped from the federal prison in Memphis by bribing a guard $50,000 to get him a guard uniform and walking out of the prison. Consequently, he became a fugitive and fled to the Bahamas and then to Medellin, Colombia. This was not his first time! In 1979 he jumped bail after being indicted in Macon, Georgia for conspiring to violate gun laws. His attorney later told the federal judge that Rosenthal was dead and produced a death certificate. Federal officials were skeptical of that, and Rosenthal was arrested in Panama.

2
Rosenthal's Criminal Background

His criminal record is well documented. He had an extensive criminal record in the state of Georgia for Auto Theft Violations, and in 1978, Rosenthal was arrested in Orlando. Upon delivery of 1,700 pounds of marijuana, he fled the country to South America to escape trial in the U.S.

In May of 1979 he and several associates were arrested in the Republic of Panama with an airplane loaded with 200 kilograms of cocaine. He was then extradited to Miami and tried in Macon for conspiracy to import the cocaine into the Middle District of Georgia.

Rosenthal was found guilty and taken to the Federal Institute in Tennessee. On September 30, 1981, Rosenthal escaped the FCI and fled to Colombia and continued his cocaine smuggling organization until September of 1983 where he was arrested by Colombian authorities and DEA.

Mona advised that Rosenthal and Steele wanted the source to assist them in the arrival of a pending shipment. Steele who was Rosenthal's lieutenant, convinced the source to start working off a debt owed to them for money, and this shipment could erase the debt.

"Mona, this is quite an opportunity to nail this group to the cross. Go ahead and tell him to alert you immediately when he gets the order to travel to Tennessee. Pick your team and get Bernie Redd, RAIC Nashville, briefed and on standby with TBI agents to assist on surveillance and arrest when load is delivered to the source and game plan for the take down once they hit the road for Florida.

"I will brief the bosses up front. This is your case and keep me posted on plans, etc. Great work, girl!"

Mona, and I go back a long way, and worked together when she was a narcotic detective with Dade Metro Sheriff's Department's Narcotic Unit! She was a case maker and great cop!

On July 1, 1982, Steele met with the source at the Varsity Restaurant in Atlanta to discuss the pending deal. Steele said that the source, would have to travel to an undisclosed location in the mountain of eastern Tennessee where the aircraft would arrive carrying the drugs and unidentified male.

Steele did not identify what the drug contents were, and the source asked what type of vehicle would be needed. Steele advised the load would be carried in a large car or station wagon. Steele advised that the Colombian on the AC would be travelling with the source to Ft. Lauderdale.

I informed Mona that she needed to ensure that she stay in contact with Country Attaché Mike Vigil, Country Attaché of Medellin, and that I would call him and give him a heads up.

I contacted Mike Vigil, a great friend and outstanding undercover agent and briefed him of the above information. We agreed that he would contact his DAS agents and establish wiretap on Rosenthal ASAP. The DAS established a phone tap on Rosenthal quickly and Mike worked with us until we together apprehended Rosenthal.

On July 11, 1982, the source was contacted by Steele to proceed to Knoxville to meet a loaded plane and transport the shipment to South Florida. Notifications went out to RAIC Bernie Redd and TBI along with the Atlanta team, and the source was surveilled checking into a motel and was instructed to park in the rear of the motel in Cleveland, TN. Surveillance was established, and a large motorhome vehicle driven by the source arrived. The source then proceeded to the room and was instructed by Mona Polen and Agent Ron Metcalf to make sure the vehicle had only a half of tank of gas and to inform the two cars' escorts, driven by Colombian males, that as soon as the load was on board, to get off at the first exit south on the interstate for gas. The suspects who drove the loads were well known by TBI agents as drug suspects.

Once loaded, the source drove off, and the escorts got off for gas refill. The source started fueling the motorhome and as predicted, the four Colombians went in to get snacks, and orders to move in were given to arrest everyone. State police and DEA groups arrested the suspects where they were, because if arrests had been made while all were in their vehicles, the two escort vehicles had machine guns on the front seats. We later learned that orders were given that if stopped by law enforcement, they were to shoot and kill the police. Arrested were nine individuals. Six of these defendants, including STEELE, were indicted on July 20, 1982, for conspiracy to import cocaine into the Eastern District of Tennessee.

To our surprise, the load was 1254 pounds of cocaine (Valued: $28,842,000)

A separate source who was cooperating with us informed us that he had attended a meeting ordered by Pablo Escobar at his office building with Rosenthal about this seizure and why it happened. The source said Pablo asked his chief of security why this occurred and why weren't security measures properly taken. According to the source, Pablo gave the nod to his bodyguard who walked behind the chief of security and shot him in the head. Pablo merely said, "Let this be a lesson to all," The meeting then ended.

From June 1982 to October 1983, the Rosenthal Organization brought in at least eighteen loads of cocaine into the United States totaling 13,000 pounds (Valued at $214.5 Million)15 of these loads, a total of 10,682 pounds became part of the Indictment, and the rest were targeted for future indictments.

Those identified at that time: Five loads were directly imported into Tennessee, two were flown into Georgia, five were flown from Colombia to the Bahamas and trans shipped to the U.S., one load came directly into the Gulf Coast of Florida, and one load was documented to be 800 pounds and was lost when the loaded aircraft crashed upon takeoff in Colombia. The last load most recently in 1983, was offloaded in the Reading, Pennsylvania area.

This in 8 months, from 1982 to 1983 amounted to 13,000 pounds of cocaine, valued at $33,000 per kilograms ($214.5 million at a purity level of 80% per kilogram).

Our investigation identified that Rosenthal's cocaine shipments were destined for delivery in South Florida to Colombian Nationals representing the Medellin supply organization. Identified Cartel member that took delivery of one of the shipment's was the son of Manuel Garces-Gonzales, Carlos Garces.

Great intelligence work helped us in identifying the members of this large organization in Medellin where Rosenthal was brokering cocaine shipments for the U.S. mob. Our surveillance work continued to identify suspects on the U.S. side, and we were able to infiltrate the Organization of Rosenthal with new sources referred to us by Law Enforcement Departments.

During a period of seven months into this investigation, one of our team agents, who will be referred to as CHICAGO to protect his identity, was able to assist in this investigation when he received a phone call from Paulding County Sheriff's Dept. He was introduced to a source of information who wished to cooperate in assisting us on the Rosenthal case. This person had been seen meeting Leonard Steele at a 7-Eleven Store in Atlanta during a surveillance of Steele.

I was advised by CHICAGO of this person, and his debriefing was interesting. This individual was an ex-Air Force officer who had a pilot working on Radar Operation on U.S. Coastal Detection and one retired from the Air Force.

He was working with Rosenthal in obtaining Pilots for

shipments of cocaine to be picked up and flown to the U.S. for the mob. His cooperation came forward after these seizures in Tennessee where Steele was arrested. The source is referred to as "P.O.S." which stands for "Perfect Original Source" in this story and for security protection.

The case became a massive investigation spanning almost three years. This became a Joint Operation with DEA offices in Atlanta, Nashville, Ft. Lauderdale, Miami, Newark, Philadelphia, New York City, Oklahoma City, Little Rock, the Bahamas, Colombia, South America, and the FBI offices in Atlanta, Ft. Lauderdale, Los Angeles, Miami, Oklahoma City, New York, Newark, Philadelphia, Little Rock, Knoxville.

In Addition, the U.S. Marshall's Service, A.T.F., The Cobb County Police Department, The Georgia Bureau of Investigations and the Tennessee Bureau of Investigation were directly involved with us.

The new source provided us with a complete breakdown of Rosenthal's drug smuggling organization and loads of cocaine picked up at hidden air strips where Escobar had delivered the shipments with his people to various U.S. states and cities. The information gave us an insight into how to operate a successful smuggling venture.

We learned from POS and established that Manuel Antonia Garces Gonzales, well known as a cartel boss, along with other high-ranking exporters, was the source of supply to Rosenthal's organization. Gonzales was the primary supplier for Rosenthal.

Rosenthal was the broker for the U.S. mob and arranged all the planning for safe transportation of cocaine shipments to the onload strip in Colombia through his cartel chief Sixto Granados Enriquez, Luis Rosendo Escobar, Alberto Escobar, and others.

Rosenthal's U.S. side of the transportation cycle in procuring load planes, pilots, rendezvous with cocaine plane arrivals at designated landing strips in the U.S. was arranged by Rosenthal's key lieutenants who were part of this conspiracy from start to finish. The lieutenants were Leonard Steele, David Alvin Warren, Carl Larry Oliver, and starting in the winter of 1982, U. S. mob members Charles Alaimo and Phillip Bonadonna.

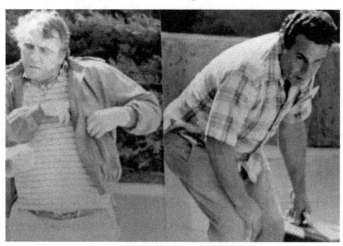

U. S. mob members Charles Alaimo and Phillip Bonadonna

Pilots and off loaders were supplied through Jackie Wayne Scarborough, David Warren, Leonard Steele, Garland Watson, Jerry Scarborough, Wilber Kidd, Lewis Crump, John Charles Bolding and William Vicary functioning as pilots for loads imported into Georgia, Tennessee, and Florida.

In addition, loads were flown from Colombia to the Bahamas and transshipped to the U.S. all arranged by Rosenthal and Artis Neely and were flown by John Robert Jones, Russell Zoellner, Sr. And Russell Zoellner, Jr. The POS informed us that the Zoellner's also had flown 1,000 pounds of cocaine into Chattanooga on August 26, 1983, and 500 pounds into Reading on September 26, 1983. Both loads had been delivered to Phillip Bonadonna and Charlie Alaimo, Carlos Alberto Herra, Robert Dunleavy, Jr., George Lombardi and others.

The involvement of organized crime figures was identified when POS was ordered by Rosenthal to meet with two individuals in Ft. Lauderdale on October 7, 1982. The source contacted Chicago and informed him of this order, and arrangements were made to conduct surveillance of this meeting by our Atlanta team and DEA Ft. Lauderdale team. The POS was instructed to check in a motel across street, and they would call him and get his room number. He was to make sure that his room faced the back of the motel facing the Port Everglades property. He was told that their names were Phil and Charlie by Rosenthal.

Chicago and part of his team was given a go to do surveillance and planned to only be stationary with no moving surveillance.

POS took a taxicab from the airport and was observed checking in to the office. The motel was one level shaped in a U and backed up to Port Everglades, which had a fence preventing anyone from entering this restricted area. The stationary surveillance was done from the airport facing Highway U.S. 1.

After a 2 hours' time, POS was observed getting into a taxi and returned to the airport to take his flight back to Atlanta. POS informed CHICAGO that they never showed up in front of his door. They knocked on the glass sliding door in the back of his room and were carrying an attaché case. They told him that they were instructed by Harold to give him $150K for purchase of an aircraft, stash house, cars and to set up a Georgia Corporation so Rosenthal/ Garces could funnel drug monies.

These two individuals had entered Port Everglades and drove to the fence line of the motel, scaled the fence, and walked to the source's back door and knocked on the glass sliding door. They left the same way after delivering the money.

After being briefed, I called our New York Office and asked to speak with Agent John Maltz who was the expert on organized crime figures. John was a great friend, and I told him we needed to ID these guys and provide their first names. Maltz said, "Frenchy, Charlie is Charles Alaimo (aka "WING"), and Phil is Phil Bonadonna, money handlers for the NY mob living in Ft. Lauderdale. You got the top guys, my man!"

"John, you're unbelievable, Pal!" Both of us laughed. We now had proof that the mob was part of this operation along with

Rosenthal. This was communicated to all, and it was getting bigger by the minute.

The source POS incorporated National Services, Inc. for Rosenthal and got the first cash delivery of $50,000 from Leonard Steele on September 5, 1982. The source received funds on Sept. 27 from Ed Tetterton, Jr. In West Palm Beach, Florida. On October 7,1982, a cash delivery of $120K from Alaimo and Bonadonna, and three more cash deliveries were made during October of 1982 totaling $449,790. POS was instructed by them to use the money to purchase a home out in the open country of Paulding County, GA, in the name of National Contract Consulting Services, Inc in late October 1982.

In November and early December of 1982, Alaimo, Bonadonna and Robert Dunleavy delivered $460,220 to undercover Agent CHICAGO and POS at the Atlanta Airport. With all the funds received, Rosenthal instructed that the POS was to purchase a Merlin 3A aircraft at the cost of $795,000.

Merlin Aircraft

The house was purchased, and arrangements were made to purchase furniture, and a large console TV at the request of Bonadonna, and two identical new 1983 Chevrolet Caprice vehicles were purchased to be load vehicles. We had time to have our technical unit install hidden microphones in the walls of every room to be able to listen to any conversation of anyone in the residence. We also installed across the street of the front residence a hidden camera in a power transformer on a telephone pole and had the camera relay TV images to our listening post one-half mile from the residence.

Our team had the new cars equipped with hidden microphones concealed in the head liners inside the cars to monitor the individuals from our surveillance aircraft and cars, once the load of cocaine was placed in the cars and driven to Ft. Lauderdale.

The command post located at an intersection was a purchased mobile home and placed on an empty lot, which we rented from the owner of this property. We observed at the intersection a small convenient store which had a pay phone booth outside. We got a court order to tap this phone line should our two mobsters use this phone for serious communication. We could directly see the occupants using the glass phone booth from the trailer. Finally, we had alerted the Paulding sheriff of our plan and assured us his full cooperation.

Between mid-December 1982 and mid-January of 1983, our Undercover Agent CHICAGO and POS met with Alaimo, Bonadonna, Dunleavy and associates, on several occasions. During these meetings, they were taken to the stash house. Arrangements had been made by them to have the house scanned for electronic bugs by a retired New York detective, who came to the house to do a sweep of all rooms and phones.

This was already predicted by us, and all bugs were wireless in nature and could be turned on and off directly from our Command Center. All listening devices were shut off and the security person cleared the house assuring them that no activity was detected.

For some reason the mobs' bosses are not rocket scientists by any means! We always got a good laugh when we dealt with them! They watched too many movies! One of our agents who worked the listening post at night, great Agent Chuck Shaming who worked for me in South Carolina, told me, "Pete if this SOB Bonadonna plays Pac-Man one more night, I'm going over there, and will shove that TV up his ass! He played all night long till 4 in the morning. All I heard all night was 'BEEP, BEEP, BEEP'!" I was laughing so hard that I almost shit myself!

During this time POS was in communication with Rosenthal and Veronica Wahl to discuss pending shipments, and our undercover agent and POS received an additional $83, 000 from Alaimo and Bonadonna.

Rosenthal also imported three shipments of cocaine into the Bahamas; the loads were 500 pounds, 600 pounds, and 500 pounds. They were flown from Colombia to the Bahamas by pilots Russel Zoellner, Sr. And Russell Zoellner, Jr., and Artis Neeley handled the storage and transshipment of all three. During this period intelligence information received indicated that Rosenthal was arranging a marine shipment of cocaine for the boat New Horizons Seaside for delivery to organized crime defendants in Los Angeles.

3
Pick Up 750 Pounds of Cocaine Worth $22.5 Million from Harold Rosenthal

February 11, 1983
Mountain Strip Medellin. Colombia

On January 27, 1983, CHICAGO and POS received a call from Rosenthal who gave POS the coordinates of the clandestine landing strip in Colombia. The load was ready for pick up. On February 9, 1983, Alaimo and William James Kielski delivered $45,000, to POS at the Paulding County residence.

The DEA undercover pilot and POS on February 10, 1983, flew from Atlanta to Aruba staying overnight and on February 11, departed Aruba for the secret strip in Colombia.

The undercover Merlin Aircraft pilot yoke had a hidden open microphone which could pick up voices once the aircraft landed and loading doors opened.

Upon landing, the doors opened, and the loading group was waiting with Rosenthal. Armed guards with machine guns surrounded the plane according to our pilot. Also present was Pablo Escobar overseeing the loading operation. Voices of our pilot were heard saying, "Nervous pistaleros walking around." We also heard duffel bags being tossed inside the aircraft. All of this was being relayed to us right to our office.

Finally, we heard POS saying, "We are good to go" as doors

closed and he sat back in the co-pilot seat. A total of 755 pounds of cocaine was onboard the plane, making this a possible dangerous takeoff. Our pilot told POS, "Hang on full throttle and hopefully we can clear the trees at the end of this strip." Rolling at full throttle, our pilot kept saying. "Come on baby, come on lift, lift." Then he suddenly said, "Miller time." This was the code word for Atlanta, here we come.

Every one of us hearing this was jumping for joy that they were safe and heading for our secret landing base at Dobbins Airforce Base in Cobb County. One of our agreements we had with the Rosenthal Group was for our pilot's security. We never disclosed where we landed in Georgia. This was accepted by all.

I was asked to go to SAIC Visnick's office where TV news announcer Forest Sawyer was present. I said to him, "Forest, got a tape of a possible smuggling operation of cocaine, possibly heading this way. The station monitors the air traffic system, and they recorded this communication which was played of our UC pilot saying Miller time."

Ray said to Sawyer that we needed for him to hold off on this and briefly swore him to secrecy and full exclusive story to him once we finished this investigation.

We trusted Sawyer Forest who always worked with us. He was amazed about this and agreed to have this kept confidential. When this operation was concluded, he had an exclusive on the story which was broadcast nationwide!

During this joint investigation, I received a middle of the night phone call from FBI counterpart Rick Dean, advising me to meet with him and his boss as soon as possible at their air wing because we needed to go to Lafayette, GA. He said that their agent in charge had just arrested a group of cocaine smugglers that had landed with a load of cocaine and that this tied in with our suspects. They briefed us on the way there and advised me that the Agent in Charge had been working this case behind their back and ours to make a name for himself. We were shocked and as we approached the hanger, we could see that the media was there, and a press conference was getting ready to be held. We told the pilot to land the chopper close to this gathering and give it full rotor once on the ground to cause a lot of wind and get people's attention. The boss Agent Toony, Rick and I approached the Agent in Charge and held a quick 'Come to Jesus meeting' with him. Agent Toony started the press conference and reported that the seizure was a tip received and resulted in this seizure. This was a close call and was shut down quickly.

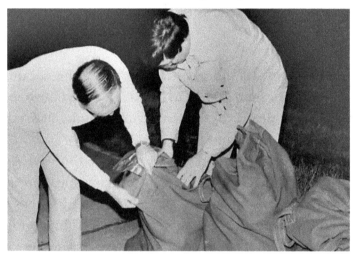

Offloading of 755 kilograms of cocaine
ASAIC Charette and RAIC Bill Malarney, Value - $26,425,000

On February 11, 1983, our undercover aircraft arrived at Dobbins Airforce Base, and the cocaine was offloaded and placed inside a van. A controlled delivery of the 755 pounds of cocaine was delivered by CHICAGO AND POS to Charles Alaimo and William Kielski who was one of the drivers for load to be delivered in Ft. Lauderdale. All our surveillance team and surveillance aircraft were on standby for the long trip to Florida the next morning.

4
Delivery and Seizure of
755 Pounds of Cocaine
Fort Lauderdale

On February 12 and February 13, 1983, the cocaine load was driven from Atlanta to Ft. Lauderdale in two separate cars, one driven by William Kielski and Christy Bryant and the other by Joseph and Rosemary Junker.

The surveillance ground group consisted of DEA, FBI, U.S. Customs and Georgia Bureau of Investigation agents. Unfortunately, arrests had to be made due to the Junker's erratic driving actions when they became suspicious of being followed by police agents. Orders were given to move in arrest them all and seize the cars and dope. This seizure had a value of $ 22.5 million.

The Junkers denied having knowledge of cocaine being in the trunk of the car and said someone had asked them, to take their car to the airport and leave it there for them to have it upon returning from a trip.

Information was gathered about them and, agents advised them that for their sake, if they were the owners of this shipment and found out they let you go, they think they would get out of town quickly. The Junkers got in a taxi and left town suddenly. The second vehicle was in Tamarac, Fl. The cocaine was retrieved and seized, and the driver was arrested.

Agent Anthony Camarato and Pete Charette open trunk of car with
duffel bags of cocaine.

Rosenthal contacted POS and told him that he needed to
have a meeting with him and Sixto Granados who was one of
Escobar's head of cocaine shipments in Barranquilla to discuss
what went wrong with this seizure. I notified our Country Attaché
of Barranquilla, Herb Williams and Mike Vagil, that the source
POS was ordered to meet Harold and Sixto. Herb was advised
the meeting would take place at the Casino Hotel and that Agent
Chicago and I would be there also since we needed to confirm
this meeting and ID Rosenthal.

Herb advised that he stay out of being there since Sixto and
his guards knew him well as the DEA boss in that city.

Sixto Granada

Agent CHICAGO and I arrived at the hotel and checked in separate rooms on the third floor. POS was told to check in on his own. Our rooms faced the front of the hotel street. The front desk of the hotel was immediately to the left as you entered and across was a restaurant /dining room that had large glass doors and glass front. To the right of the entrance was the casino which was fully packed with people. The elevator was next to the left of the casino and the restaurant. The meeting had been set for 8 p.m. at the restaurant.

At approximately 8 p.m., I observed from my hotel room window, three black SUV's turn into the street of the Hotel and park on the left curb, and the two escort vehicles front and back of the center one, eight bodyguards, who immediately surrounded the middle car, and Sixto and Rosenthal got out and were surrounded by the bodyguards who all had jackets and had in their right hands small Uzi machine guns, concealed behind the flap of their jackets.

We had planned that CHICAGO was not to be seen, and that I would go down after 30 minutes to get a newspaper and confirm that the three of them were in the restaurant then go back to my room.

It was time for me to go get the newspaper. The elevator stopped, the door opened, and I walked out Stunned by total silence. A quick look at the casino disclosed that all clients were gone, and two bodyguards stood out front of the restaurant doors. I observed Rosenthal, Sixto and POS sitting at a table having a discussion with a lit candle goblet illuminating their table with all other lights off. "Mission accomplished!" I got my newspaper from the front desk and immediately turned around to take the elevator to return to my room. The meeting lasted approximately one hour at which time I observed Sixto and Harold leaving.

We did not have any contact with POS and the next day, we left Colombia and returned to Atlanta.

5
Orders to Kill DEA Undercover Pilot

P OS was debriefed and instructed that the meeting was about their suspicion, that only one person was new in this delivery, and that was the new pilot. Orders were made by Rosenthal, Sixto and Pablo to kill the pilot and produce proof.

Our decision was to fake a killing, and have it shown in the newspapers that he died in a car accident and have copies of the article sent to Rosenthal, Sixto and Pablo. Upon seeing the news, they were satisfied.

Rosenthal continued his drug smuggling operations from March 17- September 27, 1983.

During this timeframe Rosenthal had Bonadonna, George Lombardi and Robert Dunleavy delivered $222,000 to Russell Zoellner in the Bahamas for the purchase of a Queen Air aircraft and the Zoellners flew from Dalton, GA to Colombia to pick up 1,000 pounds of cocaine that was imported into Chattanooga and was stored in a mini warehouse in Dalton, GA. It was then turned over to Charles Alaimo, Robert Dunleavy, Carlos Herrera and George Lombardi on August 29, 1983.

In September 1983, the Zoellners on Rosenthal's orders were ordered to purchase a Super DC-3 aircraft in Chica, California after receiving $ 175,000 in cash from Lombardi and Dunleavy on September 20, 1983, at the Miami Airport.

On September 25, 1983, the Zoellners flew the Super DC-3 to Colombia from Chattanooga via the Virgin Islands, returning on September 26, 1983, with 500 pounds of cocaine which was offloaded to Bonadonna, Carlos Herrera, Lombardi, Dunleavy and Alaimo in Reading.

I was contacted by Country Attaché Mike Vigil who advised me of a serious phone conversation which had occurred between Harold Rosenthal and Sixto Granados. Enriquez. Rosenthal told Sixto that the Attorney General of Colombia Laura Padilla needed to be killed. He was pushing to authorize the extradition of cartel members, and this had to be done. Sixto agreed and that it was being addressed by Pablo.

Mike advised me that this was immediately reported to the Ambassador in Bogota, and Padilla thanked us for this information and advised that he was well protected. I informed everyone of this, and sadly several days later the AG, while being driven home was assassinated by two gunmen on a motorcycle that pulled up next to his car and fatally shot him with a machine gun in broad daylight.

Mike advised us that because of the wire intercept of Rosenthal's conversation, the government immediately agreed to arrest him and extradite him to the U.S.

He also advised that we needed to plan this removal and asked for me to travel to Medellin to meet the DAS team and plan his removal. I briefed the SAIC, and HQs was briefed. I told Ray Vinsick that I would take RAIC Bill Malarney who is fluent in Spanish and U.S. Marshal Bob Darnell as part of the secret team to which he agreed, and we made immediate plans to travel to Medellin. The U.S. Attorney Larry Thompson and his case attorney Craig Gillen were briefed with Chicago. Preparations were already underway to present this case to a Federal Grand Jury.

6
Removal Planning of Harold Rosenthal's Deportation - Medellin, Colombia

September 17,1983

U pon landing in Medellin Airport, we retrieved our bags and took a taxi to our hotel. Waiting for us was Country Attaché Mike Vigil, and Agent Jose Almond. Mike had arranged for us to have a 2-bedroom suite. We went to our room and settled in, after which Mike opened his briefcase and provided us with three guns, smiling. Being armed was necessary since this town was the most dangerous place in Colombia. In other words, Welcome to Pablo Escobar Country!

In all honesty, this was an adrenaline rush for all of us, and we couldn't wait for the takedown of the most infamous American drug smuggler to be captured!

Mike advised that chief of the Anti-Drug Corps of the Colombian National Police Lt. Betancur (deceased RIP) and 9 DAS (Colombian Immigration) agents, and we were scheduled to meet with them tomorrow to begin a 'Takedown Surveillance' practice for the capture of Rosenthal.

We waited until dark to have supper outside the city to avoid detection.

Mike was one of the best undercover Hispanic agents in DEA and still a great friend.

That night the four of us in our suite had a few cervezas as we heard gunfire throughout the city. We had a big clothing armoire in the room that we moved to block the door for the night as a safety precaution. We also agreed to sleep–if that was possible–with our guns. Doing this was a must, and we agreed that if anything happened, all would die... except us! This place had no rules, and we took this seriously. It was unbelievable that all night long gunshots were heard.

We woke up the next morning and went downstairs for coffee waiting for Mike. The bellboy who had greeted us and took our bags in, waived at us, and I joked with Bill Malarney. "Bill, get the kid to come and tell him that I need to find Juan Valdez, the commercialized coffee grower and see if he can find him before we leave. I'll give him $100!"

"Frog, you are bad," he replied laughing. He called the young man who was in his late teens and communicated my message. His eyes beamed at the money to be made and would check around for me. For 10 days this poor kid worked every night looking for Valdez and pitifully informed me every day "No sé," and Bill would tell him to keep looking.

We met with Lt. Betancur and the team, and the devised plan was explained to all. Rosenthal lived on a side street from the main street that flowed through town. Everyone was assigned a partner and position on a side street to observe Rosenthal coming downhill from his residence toward the T intersection of main street which had a traffic light at the bottom. The distance was about 2 ½ blocks from Rosenthal's residence. Rosenthal always left his residence at approximately 8:00 a.m. to go to the Escobar Office Building. The plan was to have the surveillance insert themselves in front and back of Rosenthal's car and slow him down to the traffic light and make sure that the timing was in sync with the light turning red. Once stopped at the light, the team was to quickly move in and arrest him. We had a stopwatch that timed the changing of the light from green to red. We practiced this for several days until we had it in perfect timing.

On Sunday, Mike took us to a restaurant outside of town

that had an open deck overlooking spectacular mountains and canyons. We sat in a booth where Mike said, "Holy shit, guys, the guy on the other side of the bar, facing the mountains sitting at a table with a woman is Sixto Granados-Enriquez, cartel king for Barranquilla, for Pablo Escobar." He was preoccupied with his lady friend, and we had a great lunch.

7
Harold Rosenthal's Arrest
Medellin, Colombia
September 27, 1983
Last Day

This was the day that we had been waiting for over two years of fascinating work by the biggest team of federal, state and local Law Enforcement Officers in the United States.

We checked out of our hotel and our baggage boy took our bags out to the car and apologized for not being able to find Juan Valdez for me. I looked at Bill, and he looked at me with that "Come on, Frog" expression. "Bill, tell him he did a great job," and I handed him $100 and added," Proud to have met you!" This young man was beaming with enjoyment and had slight tears coming down his face. We all shook his hand and waved goodbye. What a great feeling!!

Now we learned that Sixto Granados had stayed at Rosenthal's residence Sunday night and was now going to the office driving Harold's car.

The timing worked perfectly, and the traffic light turned red as Rosenthal's car driven by Sixto was boxed in. People at the intersection on foot going to work suddenly started screaming and running for cover when they saw the team jumping out of trucks and cars running to the car at gun point to arrest Sixto and

Harold. People thought this was an assassination squad.

Harold was slowly told to get out of the passenger's side, and as I was standing facing him, he said hi to Harold showing him DEA credentials. "This is the end of the road for you, my friend. You're going home.

He just smiled and said "Okay." He was taken into custody immediately and flown to Bogota to be transported to Miami. We were asked to go to Rosenthal's residence where Lt. Betancur and his team had a search warrant and confiscated the following items:

A. Approximately 5 lbs. of cocaine
B. Approximately 2 oz. of marijuana
C. Jewelry estimated value $100,000 U.S.
D. One Ingram Machine Gun Pistol
E. One Sterling .25 Caliber Automatic Pistol
F. One Smith & Wesson .357 Caliber automatic Pistol
G. Several hundred rounds of various ammunition
H. $13,600,00 US Dollars all $100 bills
I. $2500 in American Express Checks in the name of Veronica Wahl, Rosenthal's girlfriend.
J. $700 Visa Travelers Check in the name of Veronica Wahl
K. Vast amounts of documents, including ledgers of "Harold's Drug Transactions," aerial maps of clandestine airstrips, false passports, list of phone numbers of co-conspirators, numerous photographs, etc.

Mike and Jose took us the airport, and we flew to the Bogota airport to board our plane to Miami with 3 DAS Agents who had Rosenthal in custody They were required to fly with us and once we landed, they officially turned Rosenthal to the U.S. Marshall Bob Darnell.

After taking off from Bogota, Rosenthal was seated in the rear of the plane which was closed to passengers. Harold asked if he could speak to me, so Bob Darnell asked me to come and sit with Rosenthal.

Rights administered to Rosenthal on plane

"Hi, Harold, are you all right?"

"Yes, Sir. First, I want to shake your hand. You're one ballsy man!" He extended his handcuffed right hand! "Mr. Charette, you got me fairly and a great job, but you need to get Mr. Vigil and Mr. Almon and their family out of Medellin right away. Pablo Escobar has a standing order that if the Americans attempt to remove anyone of us from here to kill them and their family. Sir, he will do it. Get word to them to leave, the sooner the better."

"Harold, Thank you. I'll be right back, I immediately informed Mike by phone and John Phelps Bogota DEA Country attaché. The agents and their families were removed, and the office shut down and never reopened.

Upon arrival in Miami, Rosenthal was turned over to U.S. Marshall Bob Darnell by the DAS Agents. Darnell advised Harold of his rights and charges lodged against him.

We took Rosenthal to the Federal Miami Detention Center. Harold was booked and incarcerated there for transfer back to the prison that he had escaped from later. Harold requested to speak to me and asked if I could get him transferred to the

Atlanta Federal Penitentiary since his wife and kids live there. I advised him that I would work on that for him and provided him with my phone number to call me to get status on that request. He thanked me and I left. I asked to speak with the director of the facility but warned him that Rosenthal needed to be watched carefully, and that my gut feeling told me he would start planning another escape, regardless of the cost. The director thanked me for the warning. We left to return to Atlanta.

L/R- Agent Bill Malarney-Marshall Bob Darnell- GS Pierre Charette

On September 29, 1983, Marshal Bob Darnel, who was in Miami, contacted me and advised that Rosenthal wished to speak with me at the Detention Center. Asst. U.S. Attorney Craig Gillen was advised and approved the meeting. Rosenthal did not want his attorney present.

I flew to Miami and met Rosenthal at the detention center conference room. Bob read him his rights, after which he signed a waiver of his rights. He was read a proffer prepared by Craig Gillen and signed it dated 9/30/1983.

Harold stated that he would consider cooperating with us because he could furnish us with large seizures of cocaine being shipped to the U.S. He further advised us those loads were normally sent from South America to the U.S. by him since he had been a broker for the U.S. Mob since his escape from prison in Tennessee. He stated that if the government could set him free and allowed him to return to South America, large seizures could be made in the U.S. He also advised us that he had been a broker for the U.S. mob since 1970 through his Uncle Al Berlin who was working for the Meyer Lansky Organization in NY. He admitted that he worked for Jack Bonadonna and could not name any others. He stated the government would have to promise not to arrest the Italians and only arrest the purchasers of the cocaine. He could not risk being a marked man by the mob since he has been accepted by the mob.

When asked "How much stuff had he sent to the U.S. in the past two years, he responded,

"You got to be kidding. I was sending not less than one shipment per week and if I did, that one shipment was not less than 300 kilograms. And I shipped on average 2-3 shipments per week and supervised all the loading of the aircrafts. These shipments were also owned by Escobar and Ochoa's and other members of the cartel."

Harold was advised that this would be discussed with us, and I would get back to him. I felt that his demands were not currently feasible. We thanked him and departed. I wasn't raised a fool! My gut instinct by reading his body language when he addressed this request was that he was lying, but I would play his game for the time being!

Returning to Atlanta was a relief, and everyone at the office was excited that we were successful in apprehending Harold.

I advised Craig Gillen that I would be recording my conversation with Harold on getting his transfer and play him so I could beat him at his own game. He agreed and laughed.

Returning to Atlanta, we received a phone call from the Miami / Ft. Lauderdale office that a source of DEA, who was in the detention center awaiting transfer, advised them that Harold Rosenthal had approached him and asked him if he knew anyone that would be willing to break him out of this facility. The source stated he knew a couple of helicopter pilots that for the right amount of money would most likely accept the job. The source got back to Rosenthal and gave him two names to put down as visitors who were related to him to be allowed to visit.

The Miami undercover agents visited Rosenthal at the detention center. Harold discussed with them that he needed to escape from this facility as soon as possible. Money to affect his escape was not an issue. Rosenthal negotiated with them, and they agreed with his plan which was to remove him from the site with a helicopter that would approach the four guard towers, shoot the guards, and land on the baseball pitcher's mound while he was on his daily scheduled one-hour exercise in the yard. He was instructed to immediately run to the helicopter and get on board. Once on board he would be flown to an awaiting speed boat a Wellcraft Scarab 30-foot boat and board it for a quick trip to the Bahamas where a plane would take him back to Colombia. They advised him that they needed money to purchase this Scarab boat as well as four kilograms of coke and $25,000 in cash for their service. Harold was in total agreement, and they provided him with the cell phone number for pickup of the money and purchase of the boat. The undercover agents were contacted by two individuals identified as Artimus Neeley and Catherine Lyons living in Hollywood, Florida who said their payment was ready to be picked up. Agents met them at this residence and were given 12 kilograms of cocaine and $20,000 in cash as instructed by Rosenthal.

Harold contacted me and ascertained from me what the status was on his transfer to Atlanta. I advised him it should be approved soon. I thought, Harold, get ready for the surprise of your life once again. Check mate!

The agents were told to go and get the boat, which was purchased by Rosenthal's people, a 30-foot Wellcraft Scarab power boat and told Harold that the removal was scheduled for tomorrow, November 18, at 5:30 p.m. Harold advised them he would be ready and easy to spot wearing an orange jumpsuit and on the pitcher's mound.

Scarab boat for escape plan

On the morning of the 18th, Harold was visited at his cell by U.S. Marshals who advised him to step out of his cell because he was being transferred to Atlanta Federal Prison.

The next day, I received a call from him. He said, "Pete, I'm in the Atlanta Pen! What happened?"

"Harold, I got it done just like you asked! The least you could say is Thank You!"

"Sorry, Pete. I appreciate you getting me here close to my family."

"Harold, I'm a man of my word! Glad I could help! Have a good day!"

I contacted the Warden Jack Handberry to meet him and brief him on our case. I advised him that based on Harold Rosenthal's history for breaking out of prison, that Harold was most likely already preparing an escape again. As predicted, he tried to plan an escape which was discovered. Consequently, he was placed in a separate section which made it impossible to escape and put on special watch.

Throughout this investigation, considerable intelligence was obtained. Based on information from knowledgeable sources, documents and data, the Rosenthal segment of the Medellin Cartel imported well over 100,000 pounds of cocaine into the U.S.

8

Southern Comfort
Federal Grand Jury Indictment

Atlanta, Georgia
55 Defendants Charged
January 23, 1984

O n January 23, 1984, Attorney General William French Smith announced in Atlanta the indictment of 30 defendants smuggling five tons of cocaine into the United States headed up by drug smuggler Harold Rosenthal. Indictments were also issued in Los Angeles, Miami, and Little Rock. A total of 25 defendants were arrested in these states.

All defendants were charged with racketeering conspiracy which carried a maximum of 20 years upon conviction in these states and $25,000 fines.

Six defendants were charged with engaging in a continuing criminal enterprise (Rosenthal, Bonadonna, Alaimo, Scarborough, Oliver, and Boldin). The statute carried a maximum penalty of life imprisonment and $100,000 fine.

Various defendants were charged with violating various drug laws such as importation of a controlled substance, conspiracy to import a controlled substance, possession with intent to distribute or distribution of a controlled substance, and interstate travel in aid in a racketeering enterprise.

Attorney General and new OCDE Task Force Coordinators

General Smith also disclosed and unsealed three related first indictments in Miami against Rosenthal, Neeley, and two others for attempted escape from a Miami detention center.

The sealed indictment was opened when Rosenthal appeared before the judge and read to Rosenthal. I was present and when the facts were read by the judge, the look on Harold's face was stunned, and he looked at me and smiled.

The judge then ordered a 15-minute break, and Rosenthal's attorney approached AUSA Craig Gillen and said, "Mr. Gillen, my client would like to say something to Mr. Charette."

Gillen answered, "No problem in my presence."

We walked to Harold who stood up, handcuffed, and spoke. "Pete, I want to shake your hand. You're one smart man! You're good and played me well."

"Harold, I appreciate your honesty and praise and wish you the best. Checkmate!" We both shared a laugh. That moment was priceless and coming from this man was a hell of a ride finally coming to an end soon.

Rosenthal was found guilty on all charges and is serving a life sentence.

The indictment in Little Rock found Bonadonna and Alaimo along with 11 others guilty for conspiring to import heroin and marijuana.

The third indictment in Los Angeles found 13 persons including Alaimo, Rosenthal, and Bonadonna guilty for conspiring to import marijuana from Colombia to the states.

The indictment also charged Rosenthal for trying to arrange the murders of U.S. and Colombian law enforcement agents after he was arrested in Colombia in 1983.

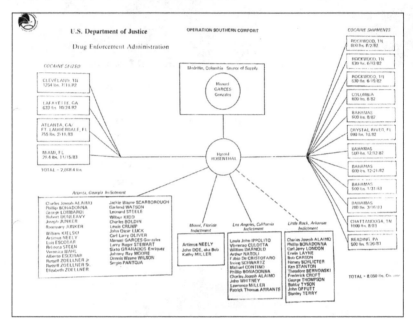

Rosenthal's Drug Organization

The Southern Comfort case was the most impressive operation ever undertaken in this country. The teamwork by all involved (See Appendix) was one that showed that by working together, the results are massive and rewarding. Until this day, I think about what a great career it was to have been a law enforcement officer working around the world and gaining so many great friends along the way.

Was the work dangerous? Of course, it was both a dangerous and exciting job, and I would do it all over again! I achieved my dream to be a good undercover agent and to have worked with the best agents in FBN/BNDD/DEA.

I have but one regret. SAIC Raymond Vinsick and I had nominated numerous agents for the Attorney General Award of the Year and who were well deserving of this honor. But because of internal politics within the top of command, our nominations were denied. We insisted that a certain person's name needed to be in the nomination process. Ray and I refused to include the name since no direct involvement took play in this case by this person. We both agreed that this was internal political hypocrisy and as a result, no one received this deserved honor and recognition of the highest award of the Department of Justice. This was like a stab in our backs to deny these great agents who made this case possible and brought it to a successful conclusion.

Fortunately, there was one man who recognized this hysterical case as deserving of recognition. This great man was Ross Perot (RIP), chairman of the Texas War on Drugs group in Dallas. Mr. Perot once ran for President. We were advised that Mr. Perot wanted to honor the administrator of DEA along with SAIC Ray Vinsick, Pierre Charette, Agents Tommy Thompson and Ron Metcalf and our spouses to be the guests of honor at a sit-down banquet for our efforts on Southern Comfort. The banquet was attended by well-known Texans and Dallas Cowboy players.

We all met at the entrance door of the banquet room. Jack Lawn was standing with his wife, and I greeted him and started to introduce my wife Janice when Jack said, "My God, Janice!" And hugged her along with his wife who also was excited to see her. All of us were stunned.

"Excuse me, do you two know each other?" I asked laughing.

Jack responded, "Pete, Janice was our secretary in the FBI office in Augusta. She typed all my reports."

I was stunned but we all had a great evening together. Mr. Perot spoke and praised us for our work and presented each of us with a specially made Cold Combat .45 Masterpiece, each numbered one to four in a beautiful glass beveled mahogany box.

This gift was authorized by President Ronald Reagan. I have received numerous offers from gun collectors and turned them all down.

One other dignitary also recognized my 20 years of service with DEA and that was Attorney General of the United States, Ms. Janet Reno.

The award refusal was done by the previous administration and has always left a bad feeling in my heart.

We all met with Mr. Perot a year later. I was exiting his headquarters with three agents for lunch and a taxi was letting off a passenger. It was Ross Perot coming to meet with Jack Lawn. He walked toward us and said, "Pete Charette, how are you?"

"Mr. Perot, I'm doing well, sir." Then I introduced my colleagues and wished him a great day. The man was amazing and down to earth. (RIP)

I would like to end by saying that this is a great profession and an honorable one. I leave my family and grandchildren with this great legacy and all of you who shared this incredible ride with me.

Office of the Attorney General
Washington, D. C. 20530

November 26, 1993

Mr. Pierre A. Charette
Assistant Special Agent In Charge
Drug Enforcement Administration
Miami Field Division
8400 N.W. 53rd Street
Miami, FL 33166

Dear Mr. Charette:

I want to offer my sincere appreciation for your 20 years of loyal and dedicated service to the Drug Enforcement Administration. I realize that the retirement of any dedicated professional such as yourself evokes bittersweet emotions; however, you should look back upon the previous 20 years with the satisfaction that you have played a major role in DEA's effort to rid our society of drugs. No greater public service can be offered than a career in law enforcement.

I wish you all the best in the coming years and hope that you have a healthy and happy retirement.

Sincerely,

Janet Reno

Copy of Janet Reno's letter

May God bless our police worldwide! Be safe and thank you, God, for being my guardian throughout these 33 years. Thank you to all my supporters for allowing me to take this ride and to take you on this journey.

LOVE YOU ALL,
PETE

About the Author

This is the story of a French-Canadian boy whose name is Pierre "Pete" Charette, born in Valleyfield, Quebec Province, and who became a historical figure in the war on drugs in the United States and Europe. His adventures spanned a heart-pounding 33 years as a police officer, undercover detective and DEA Special Agent throughout the United States and around the world. It chronicles Charette's fascinating, high-stakes and impactful career first-hand. It includes some of the most famous cases ever developed by him, his colleagues and the DEA.

His investigative ability and imagination in numerous undercover roles, took him from the United States into the French criminal underworld (including the French Connection), the Iron Curtain, and the southern United States to uncover some of the most famous drug cases in U.S. history. His life is filled with cunning intrigue and white-knuckle courage, risking his life on numerous occasions, in order to effect the arrest of these major international drug traffickers.

Throughout his career, this special agent received numerous awards for his bravery and accomplishments in the war on drugs against the United States. In this book, Charette offers first-hand accounts of investigations that have paved the path for the development of new and innovative techniques for undercover work and investigations in narcotic enforcement.

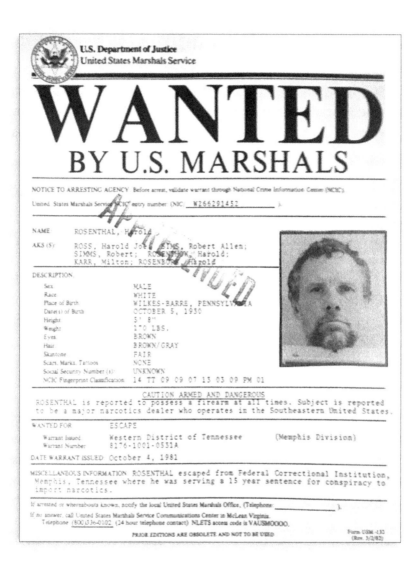

Rosenthal's Wanted Poster "Apprehended!!"

Appendix

The success of this case was done by an entire team of agents and police officers in numerous states. Without the combined teamwork of these great officers, this case would never have reached the highest level of any narcotic case ever made in the history of law enforcement.

I need to pay tribute to each one of these teams' members since this was a team effort and proved to be such a success.

SAIC Ray Vinsick (deceased), ASAIC Art Carter

Atlanta:

GS/ Criminal Investigator (OCDETF) Coordinator, Southeast Drug Taskforce Pierre" Pete" Charette,

GS/ James P. Guy (deceased RIP "JIM" my dear friend!), Agents: Mona Polen, Harold Metcalf (deceased RIP),

Chicago:

James Myles, Bennie Swint, Larry Sproat, Don Augustine, Tammy Connelly RAIC William Malarney (deceased RIP my good friend. Miss you Pal!) Country Attaché Mike Vigil, S/A Joe Almons, S/A Carl Chaves, S/A Ron Pettingill, Intelligence Supervisor, Tyrone Von Yarn, Tom Kist, Ludlow Adams, Gene Bachman, GS Bernie Redd, Buster Griggs, Kelley Goodowens, Chuck Schaming, Gerald Chapman, Chuck Crane, Jim Williams, Tom Kist, Don Augustine, Robert Michelotti, Robert Johnson, Ludlow Adams, Caesar Diaz, William Kieling, Van Quarles, Rick Tucker, Ray Stastny (deceased RIP, *"Best Agent and "HERO" who died for his country on the job"*) Steve Peterson, Ray Murry, Mike Huerta, James Dobson, IA Marty Pierce, Judith Metcalf, Analyst.

Secretaries:

Shirley Brown, Andrew Hey, Gloria Smith, Gail Williams, Rene Clark, Deborah Title

Air Wing Supervisors:

Ludlow Adams, Atlanta, Joe Bock Miami Division, Undercover Pilot Michael Leonard, ATF S/A William Steed

Ft. Lauderdale :

RAIC Paul Terese , Tony Camarato, GS Tony Amoraso, FBI Agent Larry Harrigan, GS Jack Toal, S/A's Steve Georges, William Ledwith, Mike Garland, Don Carter, Ron Davis

Atlanta FBI:

SAC Larry York, OCDETF Coordinator Rick Dean, GS- Bill Whitley, S/A Fred, Ruhlman, ASAC Carol Tooey, Charles Moore

Miami Florida Joint Task Force:

GS/ Tom Smith. S/A Ron Davis, S/A Don Carter,

DEA Little Rock, Arkansas:

RAIC Gary Wardon

DEA New Orleans:

RAIC Gary Warden, S/A Michael Hurley, S/A John Hughes, S/A James D. Boyce

DEA Newark, NJ:

RAIC Michael Tobin, GS/ Matthew J, Maher, S/A's: Ron Catanese, Alexander Gourley, Ulises; Delgado, Brian Collier, Michael Statlander

DEA Atlantic City:

RAIC Gerard Moore, S/A John Smith

US ATTORNEY Atlanta:

Larry Thompson,

AUSA's: Craig Gillen, Steve Wisebram, James Deichert

Organize Crime Strike Force, Atlanta:

US. Marshall - Atlanta

Agent Robert Darnell, Lynn Duncan, Winford Griffen

US CUSTOMS Atlanta:

Paul Reed

IRES—Atlanta

S/A Steve Sachs, S/A Del Butler GBI

Charles A. Sever, Carl Neely, John Lang

Federal Prison Atlanta, GA:

Warden Jack Hanberry

CPSIA information can be obtained
at www.ICGtesting.com
Printed in the USA
BVHW080351021022
648350BV00001B/31

9 781955 944960